ART AND ANALYSIS

AN ADRIAN STOKES READER

T0345603

ART AND ANALYSIS

AN ADRIAN STOKES READER

Edited by
Meg Harris Williams

Published for
The Harris Meltzer Trust
by
KARNAC

Published in 2014 for The Harris Meltzer Trust
by Karnac Books Ltd, 118 Finchley Road, London NW3 5HT

British Library Cataloguing in Publication Data
A C.I.P. for this book is available from the British Library

ISBN 978 1 78220 118 2

Edited, designed and produced by The Bourne Studios
www.bournestudios.co.uk
Printed in Great Britain

www.harris-meltzer-trust.org.uk
www.karnacbooks.com

CONTENTS

ACKNOWLEDGEMENTS

Acknowledgements are due to the Estate of Adrian Stokes for permission to reprint selections from his writings and the cover image, and to the Tate Gallery for the cover photograph. Donald Meltzer's biographical note on Adrian Stokes (Appendix 1) was first published in *Contemporary Psychoanalysis* (1974); Eric Rhode's introduction to Stokes' collected papers in *A Game That Must Be Lost* (Appendix 2) was first published by Carcanet Press (1973) .

I would particularly like to thank both Telfer Stokes and Eric Rhode for encouragement, help and advice.

Adrian Durham Stokes was born in Bayswater, London, in 1902, and died in Hampstead, London, in 1972. He was educated at Rugby and at Magdalen College, Oxford, and was a member of the Euston Road School of artists during the 1930s, when he also undertook psychoanalysis with Melanie Klein. He was an athlete in his youth and after a period of travel and journalism became both a painter and a writer on aesthetics, focusing on Italian Quattrocento art and architecture, Impressionist painting, Russian ballet and Greek culture.

During the war years he lived near St Ives in Cornwall. He became a trustee of the Tate Gallery in 1961 and rescued the work of Alfred Wallis, the Cornish primitive, from oblivion. Many distinguished figures of his time in the fields of art, philosophy and psychoanalysis were among his personal friends and considered him one of the most original and creative writers on art, in the English aesthetic tradition of Ruskin and Pater. Stokes married twice and had three children.

Among the twenty books he published in his lifetime are: *The Quattro Cento* (1932), *Stones of Rimini* (1934), *Tonight the*

Ballet (1934), *Colour and Form* (1937), *Venice: An Aspect of Art* (1945), *Cézanne* (1947), *Inside Out* (1947), *Art and Science* (1949), *Smooth and Rough* (1951), *Michelangelo* (1955), *Raphael* (1956), *Greek Culture and the Ego* (1958), *Monet* (1958), *Three Essays on the Painting of Our Tim*e (1961), *Painting and the Inner World* (including a dialogue with Donald Meltzer) (1963), *The Invitation in Art* (1965), and *Reflections on the Nude* (1967). He also published numerous articles and reviews.

A selection of his writings edited and introduced by Richard Wollheim was published as *The Image in Form* (1972). After his death, Stokes' further papers were collected and introduced by Eric Rhode in *A Game That Must Be Lost* (1973); his poems were collected and introduced by Peter Robinson, entitled *With All The Views* (1981). Most of his writings were subsequently collected in the three-volume *Critical Writings* (1978), edited by Lawrence Gowing.

Biographical and bibliographical information, together with a list of Stokes scholars and works, may be found on the Adrian Stokes website: www.pstokes.demon.co.uk.

Meg Harris Williams read English at Cambridge and Oxford universities and is a visual artist and writer with a lifelong psycho-analytic education; her mother was Martha Harris of the Tavistock Clinic and her stepfather Donald Meltzer. She is a visiting lecturer for the Association of Group and Individual Psychotherapists and for the Tavistock Clinic, where Stokes is included in one of her teaching modules on applied psychoanalysis.

Her books are: *Inspiration in Milton and Keats* (1982), *A Strange Way of Killing: Emily Bronte's Wuthering Heights* (1987), *The Apprehension of Beauty* (with Donald Meltzer, 1988), *The Chamber of Maiden Thought* (with Margot Waddell, 1991), *A Trial of Faith: Hamlet in Analysis* (1997, new edition 2014), *The Vale of Soulmaking: the Post-Kleinian Model of the Mind* (2005), *The Aesthetic Development: The Poetic Spirit of Psychoanalysis* (2010), and *Bion's Dream: A Reading of the Autobiographies* (2010). Website: www.artlit.info.

Meg Harris Williams

E ver since Richard Wollheim's *Image in Form* fell out of print, so well-thumbed that its acid-soaked Penguin leaves have long ago disintegrated, there has been a need for some sort of taster or introduction for new students to the work of Adrian Stokes. Adrian Durham Stokes (1902-1972) was an "English aesthete" in the tradition of Ruskin and Pater,[i] and, like others in that rare tradition, highly individual and idiosyncratic in his approach and writing style. As a philosopher of art more than an art critic, his writing appealed to practising artists to an unusual extent; he was himself a painter and many of his pictures are held by the Tate. His earlier writings were explorations of aesthetic experience founded on architecture and landscape, in particular that of Italy, then expanded to include sculpture and, subsequently, the art of painting. Although his focus moved on, his vision of the fundamental mind-feeding experience offered by all these subjects never changed. But it did develop conceptually, and the most significant factor in this was his psychoanalytical experience, which

---

i See David Carrier, *The English Aesthetes* (1997).

began in earnest in 1930 when he commenced a seven-year personal analysis with Melanie Klein.[ii] As a result, Stokes (as Donald Meltzer has said) built a bridge between art and psychoanalysis "that will stand for generations", adding that although Stokes himself did not expound his aesthetic theory in a final form, Wollheim's selection nonetheless "pulled it together" for readers (Meltzer, 1974): that is, it demonstrates its shape, consistency and evolution in publications that spanned more than four decades. Subsequent scholars have always been impressed by the integrity of Stokes' aesthetic-psychoanalytic worldview, which was innate in him, whilst finding an answering echo and confirmation in Kleinian psychoanalytic theory as it was developing during the last century. As Wollheim observed, there seemed already to have been a "place reserved" in Stokes' mind for Mrs Klein's ideas, hence it was a natural gravitation; and through the Imago Society[iii] and other friendships, Stokes kept closely in touch with the subsequent evolution of these ideas.

The collection of extracts in this book is less comprehensive than Wollheim's, and it does not attempt to encompass, or even to dip into, the full range of Stokes' interests. Nor can this brief introduction offer an overview of the body of Stokes scholarship, which bears witness to an increasing appreciation of his methodology and vision and includes new editions of some

---

ii   With regard to Stokes' approach to psychoanalysis, Eric Rhode has written (personal communication): "In his early twenties he went to Italy with his parents and the beauty of Liguria awoke a passion in him for the beauty of the visual arts. In those days travel around Italy was not easy, but this did not discourage the young Stokes from visiting remote sites and rediscovering great paintings in inaccessible farmhouses. He was enchanted by Urbino. The Sitwells, Ezra Pound and D. H. Lawrence in turn befriended him and encouraged his writing. He entered a state of depression in part but only in part stimulated by the death of Lawrence, and a friend who was in psychoanalysis suggested he should seek out Ernest Jones who at that time had encouraged Melanie Klein to come to London to analyse his son. Jones referred Stokes to Mrs Klein who had a practice in Notting Hill Gate."

iii   Co-founded with the musician Robert Still in 1950; members included Richard Wollheim, Donald Meltzer, Wilfred Bion, Roger Money-Kyrle, John Oulton Wisdom, and Stuart Hampshire (see Meltzer, 1974 [below, Appendix 1]; Glover, 2009, p. 86.)

works. The relatively restricted intention here is to convey the quality of Stokes' vision of the linkage between aesthetic experience and psychoanalysis: meaning not just psychoanalytic theory, but an awareness of unconscious emotional patterns and resolutions manifest in art-forms that is heightened or clarified by psychoanalytic experience – sometimes, indeed, in spite of psychoanalytic theory, at least in its original reductive approach to art and the artist. In particular, the aim is to make accessible Stokes' personal model of engaging with what the poets call "the idea of the beautiful", and to bring out its psychoanalytic relevance; for his best writing has a poetic aura and, as always in poetry, his personal way of "close looking" is both idiosyncratic and universal.

It is in Stokes' later writings (the Tavistock series of books) that we find his most deliberate moves toward formulating a deeply psychoanalytic theory of aesthetic experience, especially in relation to his establishment of the parallels between the two Kleinian "positions" ("paranoid-schizoid" and "depressive") and the two approaches to art ("carving" and "modelling") which apply to artist and art-viewer alike: the depressive entailing an acceptance of the object's otherness and the self's dependence upon it for mental sustenance; the paranoid-schizoid representing a more primitive desire to possess, control and merge with the object. For through his knowledge of Kleinian object-relations theory, as Nicky Glover writes:

> Stokes became well equipped to address the interplay between the artist and his medium, together with the relationship between the spectator-critic and the artwork. Indeed, in his approach, Stokes saw no essential difference in the relationship between artist and medium, and spectator and artwork, for, according to Kleinian theory, the same intrapsychic processes are at work in *all* object relationships. (Glover, 2009, p. 87)

Stokes himself said there was no essential (psychic) difference between the artist and the art-appreciator; he was interested in aesthetic response in the widest sense of the human need to have meaningful experiences by means of the outer world of "objects" which could then contribute to inner-world structure – to the development of mind and personality. It was natural to him to fuse his personal, innate vision of beauty with the Kleinian model of the mind in which, for the infant, the mother is the world, arousing ambivalent emotions of love and hate which are only resolvable through an attempt to get to know the aesthetic object (its inside as well as its outside), not intrusively but respecting its otherness: this being the only real means of seeking self-knowledge and proceeding with psychic development.

The Kleinian, or post-Kleinian, implications of this view were later clarified theoretically by Meltzer (1988) in his formulation of the "aesthetic conflict" that occurs in relation to the tension between the visible external beauty of the object, and the object's unknown internal qualities, space or intentions which cannot be sensuously apprehended: thus two ways of knowing are brought into conflict. The prototypal external reality of the mother is echoed in the ambivalent emotional impact with which the self initially confronts a new idea, whose potential "beauty" arouses fear and apprehension as well as attraction. As the art philosopher Susanne Langer suggested: [iv]

> Aesthetic attraction, mysterious fear, are probably the first manifestations of that mental function which in many becomes a peculiar tendency to see reality symbolically, and which issues in the power of conception, and the lifelong habit of speech. (Langer, 1942, p. 110)

The tension between contrary emotions stimulates the need to find a symbol that contains the meaning.

For Stokes, the ultimate aesthetic object that arouses our sense of awe and wonder is the world itself; and the initial aesthetic object is the mother, in both the emotional and the bodily sense, initially in the part-object form of the breast. The relationship with the breast is the foundation for the quest for self-knowledge, and art is one of the supreme modes of exploring and modelling this quest. As he describes in his autobiography *Inside Out*, and as may be seen from his other writings,

---

iv   Stokes refers to Langer's *Feeling and Form* in *Michelangelo* (1955), n. 275.

the "good mother" held in his childhood preconceptions became realized or actualized on his first encounter with the world of the Mediterranean – its landscape, its art, its lifestyle, and even its geological prehistory; all of which contribute to the fantasy of the qualities of the internal object – its richness, capaciousness, stability. This contrasted with his picture of a deprived mother, vulnerable to schizoid attacks – a "real" fantasy depicted through observations or memories of life in London's Hyde Park. David Carrier, in his introduction to the narrative, explains:

> Stokes is telling his life story by redescribing the contrast, presented in his 1930s books about fourteenth-century Italian sculpture, between modelled works which reveal tension and that ideal carved art which is atemporal . . . Going to Italy, he develops in ways Klein gave him the vocabulary to understand. (Carrier, 1997, p. 14)

Indeed if we follow Stokes' own emphasis on unconscious thinking, we can say that in terms of mental structure he already "understood", but then found a verbal congruence in the ideas of psychoanalysis.

The concept of the restoration of the good mother is the foundation for Stokes' declaration that successful art is a representation of "sanity", and that likewise, sanity is "an aesthetic achievement". He defines the "essence of sanity" as the power to communicate and receive communications. Sanity – health, wholeness – is the artist's goal in approaching the innate but hidden object-potentialities of his material. The insistence on the idea of "sanity" countermands the too-frequent psychoanalytic assumption that art is significant for its revelation of the artist's personal psychoses and that herein lies its interest for psychoanalysis. In Stokes's view, by contrast, immersion in an artwork may well put the artist (or viewer) in touch with their psychosis, since elements of aggression must be activated in order to start moving out of inchoateness; and these elements always remain visible within the finished work. But if the work is successful then it *must* present an image of sanity – in which all these destructive or hateful elements encounter not denial but rather, transformation, under the greater aegis of the "good object". As the sculptor Louise Bourgeois engraved on the lintel of one of her installations (*Precious Liquids*): "Art is a guarantee of sanity." It is not the psychosis that is interesting, but the integration of psychoses and compulsions within the greater art-symbol.

All underlying form is "of the body", writes Stokes: whether the subject under consideration be nature, the manmade environment, art or architecture. This is the basis of our human perception and provides the meaning which we attribute to the outer world. We see "the body" in nature as much as in the manmade environment and its contents. Stokes initially talked of "the emblematic", then later came to call this complex compositional network "the image in form", directing attention to the *underlying form* of the artwork which has an organized meaning of its own, as distinct from its *content* or apparent subject: a meaning which the artist may only realize (consciously or unconsciously) as the work nears completion. With regard to "the image in form", Eric Rhode writes:

> [Stokes] thought that the contemplation of art encourages the spectator to recognize the "total configuration as a symbol" through the structure of what he called "the image in form". And he believed that the contemplation of art, even more than the contemplation of landscape, could bring the spectator to an intuitive understanding of how the often inchoate self might identify with those internal figures that psychoanalysts call "good objects". (Rhode, 1973, p. 4)

The "image in form" is equivalent to Langer's definition of the "underlying idea" of a work, or the "art-symbol" – that is, the overall symbol, not the various subsidiary symbols which may be featured like signage within the composition. The overall symbol is not a reference but a container, comprised of all the significant formal elements such as composition, colour, texture, media handling, etc. As Stokes explains in his essay on "Primary process, thinking and art":

> The shapes at which [a person] looks, whatever the object of his immediate attention, are bound to encounter the inner

landscape. I have not in mind here the perception of a phallic symbol, say, in a tree, but the impingement of the total configuration as a symbol, an aspect of symbolization *vis-à-vis* the outside world at large to which psychoanalysts are not inclined to pay prolonged attention even when attending to matters of art. (Stokes, 1973, p. 116)

This recognition of underlying form (in literary studies known as "deep grammar") melts down the rigidity of the classical psychoanalytic contrast between primary (unconscious) and secondary (conscious) processes, which becomes of far less relevance once the art-process is recognized as one of unconscious thinking finding symbolization in a way that is communicable to others. In the same paper Stokes makes use of recent psychoanalytic and philosophical ideas to fortify the view that unconscious and non-verbal fantasies may be highly sophisticated in their structure, to a degree that is not only deeper than purely intellectual formulation, but also in greater contact with the underlying good mother or object, and less the instrument of childish omnipotence.

The search for underlying form by means of immersion in the outwardness and corporeality of the artmaking process is carried out by projective and introjective identifications (in psychoanalytic terms), through which the inner object relates to the outer object or artwork. Stokes notes the dialectical structure of all philosophical quests: two basic principles or positions are required, which need first to be distinguished, and then integrated. Making use of his psychoanalytic knowledge, he expanded existing aesthetic theories of carving and modelling, and of identity-in-difference, by adding in the concept of identification. He applied this to the two fundamental modes of object-relationship operating in aesthetic experience: otherness and fusion, separateness and possession, the whole-object and the part-object viewpoints. On this basis he could vividly observe and describe the interaction of different psychic approaches to art, and the way in which they paralleled the child's complex bonding processes with its mother, "working-out" (in his loaded term) the often disturbing and conflictual beginnings of aesthetic absorption.

Stokes' lifelong preoccupation with the dialectical modes increased in complexity over the span of his writings. Initially the terms carving and modelling had referred to the difference between stone- and bronze-sculpting, insofar as these represent different ways of attempting reparation of the aesthetic object that is inevitably damaged the instant its surface is disturbed by the sculptor. Where carving, after its initial attack, supremely avows the independent otherness of the object, entailing relinquishment and respect for its inviolacy or privacy, modelling gives play to primitive types of fusion and part-object projections into the object, together with the infantile temptation of the self to believe it is an omnipotent creator in full control of its productions.

In his early works, Stokes used the term "Quattro Cento" to epitomize the quintessential carving approach, since he associated or discovered it through the stone carved-out sculpture of the Quattrocento. He distinguished it from building-up (modelling) methods of reparation of the object, as used in other types of sculpting and which are also typical of the medium of painting. When he became interested in expanding his aesthetic from the realm of sculpting to that of painting, he incorporated "identity in difference" into his vocabulary, since he needed to find a way to describe the painter's equivalent to the sculptor's carving during the search for a "total configuration" – an overall symbol not just a part-object symbol. Identity in difference encompassed colour, shape and composition, and the relation of parts to the whole on a flat surface, not just a three-dimensional one. As a result of this expansion in his focus, the artist's mental orientation was no longer tied or confined to any particular medium but became, as Glover puts it, more "existential": concerned with abstract modes of being that are applicable to any activity or situation in the outside world.

For a long time, Stokes maintained the "Quattro Cento" or carving was his "preferred" mode. Gradually however, as his scope and knowledge-base widened, he came emphatically to assert that both orientations are present in all aesthetic experience, and are indeed necessary and complementary: carving does not negate or devalue modelling but rather, subsumes it. He saw the rhythm of attack and reparation, and the oscillation of paranoid–schizoid and depressive orientations, as part of the life instinct, fundamental both to artistic creativity and to psychic development. The self-sufficient object was modified – and ultimately enriched – by acknowledging the usefulness of "envelopment" and the intermingling of minds. Pursuing this theme more closely, it became apparent that this intermingling could take on either aggressive or enquiring qualities, in a way that the post-Kleinian theory of Bion and Meltzer has categorized as a distinction between "intrusive projective identification" and "communicative projective identification". Bion indeed saw the latter as alternating between "patience" (a stressful state) and "security" (a momentary glimpse of truth); and to indicate this oscillation he coined the symbol Ps<–>D, a psychoanalytical equivalent to the alternation of modelling and carving modes in artistic process; while by contrast, intrusive identification results in a cynical state of mind which is out of touch with emotion and represents a tyrannical attack on the link between self and object. Bion's theory of the positive emotional links between love, hate and knowledge, as distinct from non-emotional, cynical or negative links, allowed for the pre-Kleinian pain-pleasure principle to be superseded, along with the view of art as the sublimation of repressed guilt-ridden desires. Instead it is a quest for sanity through symbolizing the interaction of identifications, marking out the route toward self-knowledge.

For the artist, all these identifications are captured and displayed in the underlying bodily form of the artwork, whose final equilibrium contains and manifests the processes of its composition. The achievement of formal unity or harmony – "the image in form" – corresponds to the depressive acceptance of the otherness of the aesthetic object, an acceptance which is only gained after an initial carving attack on the medium and a sequence of modelling moves aimed at establishing not omnipotent restitution but communicative links. So the artwork is to the viewer – and indeed to the artist, who is the servant not the master of his own creativity – a symbolic container for the emotional turbulence, though not in the sense of a comforter (as the multi-functional external mother may be); rather, as Keats describes it in the "Grecian Urn", the aesthetic object regains an inviolate psychic distance after the incursions of the child: an enriched wholeness after projection and introjection have achieved a fine balance.

To conclude on a personal note: I first became acquainted with the writings of Adrian Stokes at a time when I was searching for an aesthetic theory which could encompass the notion of literary criticism as an art form, and was feeling impatient and disillusioned with the reductionist theories in fashion during the 1980s, including many of those which purported to be psychoanalytic. I was heartened and inspired by reading Stokes' magnificent study of Turner, which seemed to offer a genuine interdisciplinary bridge, not just in discursive terms but in the poetic language of a lived experience attained through finding a "symbolic congruence" with the aesthetic object. At that time I wrote:

> We are looking for an approach to the body of art – the Urn – which expresses a congruence with the tensions and directives of its underlying Idea, its commanding form: an approach which is the opposite of reductive, and which in a sense partakes of the art-symbol's integrity and echoes its world-of-its-own. On one level, Stokes gives a "Kleinian interpretation" of art; but it is not one which is founded principally on categorizing art's phantasy contents, still less on the evaluation of psychopathology (which he regarded as a sad travesty of the "transcendent" or "effervescent" or "widely significant" psychoanalytic spirit). Nor does he rely solely on the other critical favourite, on tracing the motif of "reparation" – the Kleinian restatement of the traditional theme of innocence beyond experience – though he is indeed continuously aware of the rhythm of attack and reparation, and of the artist's anxiety at confrontation with a blank sheet of paper where the first step in creation is violation. But Stokes' major stance for investigation is his architectural sense of worlds within

worlds, of three-dimensional structures, spatial volumes and lines of force, which he recognizes as dramatizing psychic tensions. In particular he focuses on the resonance between inside and outside, where the dual functions of envelopment and incorporation – the essence of aesthetic appreciation – takes place. Thus he describes simultaneously both the reconstitution of the "independent, self-sufficient, outside good object", and our relationship with it as it evolves through "contemplating and following out" its formal network of directions: the way in which we become "in touch with a process that seems to be happening on our looking, a process to which we are joined as if to an alternation of part-objects." (Williams, 1988, pp. 187-188)[v]

The "aesthetic criticism" that Stokes here demonstrates so vividly is the closest that criticism comes to the transference conditions of psychoanalysis, modelling the most intimate and essential of analogies between the two disciplines. As Wollheim has observed, Stokes – like Ruskin – has "a precision not of description, but rather of presentation, as though the critic's task was to offer up, along with the object, those associations and sentiments which determine its place in our understanding or appreciation" (Wollheim, 1972, p. 30). Stokes' prose, at its best, is indeed a "presentational form", in the sense formulated by Susanne Langer; its meaning is in its deep grammar, not in the lexical sign-language of its phraseology. It demands that we become enveloped in a way analogous to his own envelopment by his theme: that is, it works by initiating identifications, not by dictate. Lawrence Gowing said that the experience of reading Stokes was very close to looking at art – and he saw this as an unusual feature, unlike most art criticism. And it is perhaps an illusion that we can read for ourselves: we are always hand in hand like Dante with Virgil, whether with internal or external objects, attempting to fit our minds to the experience on offer. Symbolic congruence is a generative mode, based on inspiration rather than imitation: by its means a potentially infinite series of transformations may be transmitted between

v   An internet version of this paper, "A post-Kleinian model of aesthetic criticism", is available on www.psyartjournal.com.

reader-subject and landscape- or artwork-object, in a way analogous to Meltzer's description of the psychoanalytic process as a "conversation between internal objects". It is what enables psychoanalysis to join the ranks of the art-forms in what Stokes calls the spirit of "brotherliness", rather than pronouncing judgement on the working of artists.

Through his distinctive prose style we see Stokes discovering his own emotional experience as he looks-and-writes, communicating in minute detail the struggles of creativity. By "working-out" in this way (to use his own phrase) he models for the reader his personal explorations into the truth of beauty, "travelling in the realms of gold" as Keats put it. Although this type of acutely observed immersion in the aesthetic object is generally unknown to most psychoanalytic writers on the arts, it is quintessentially psychoanalytic. In fact this ultimately provides the most vital link between Stokes' ideas and those of psychoanalysis: the translation of an inside-outside dialogue into a verbal art-form which then demands from the reader a generative response of symbolic congruence – not colonizing but internalizing.

With this in mind, the selections in this book are arranged not chronologically, but with a view to first establishing Stokes' philosophical and psychoanalytic theoretical viewpoint, using shorter extracts, and ending with longer passages that demonstrate the power of his capacity for close observation and description. Subtitles for each excerpt are taken from Stokes' own words, with the exception of "catastrophic change" for the Giorgione (Stokes' term is "interchange"), as his description fits so well the classical term which was adopted by Bion to express the ambivalent qualities of imminent psychic change.

Chapter One, "The quest for sanity", establishes the general sense in which the underlying desire for reparation of the mother is equivalent to the development of sanity, something which Stokes considers "an aesthetic achievement". It is dependent on the establishment of communication between self and internal object. The kind of "communion" searched for entails more than one mode and transcends the simplistic division of conscious-unconscious, secondary-primary; it entails learning to read depth arguments and symbols, not just surface ones. Hence the special quality of "contemplative states" which are both inward and outward-looking.

Chapter Two, "Art and the inner world", explores these themes in more detail, emphasizing the Kleinian view of the concreteness of the inner world and how it is mirrored in the outer world, not in the sense of the pathetic fallacy, but in the sense of how we attribute meaning to the actuality that we perceive – indeed how our perceptions are created in tandem with these inner (Platonic) pre-conceptions. This chapter and the previous one include extracts from a dialogue with Donald Meltzer on what art shows us about the nature of the inner world; the role of the artist in society is considered and the idea of the "bad object" is clarified as being a projection of bad parts of the self; and the essential psychic similarity between the artist and the art-appreciator is established.

Chapter Three, "Modes of art and modes of being", collects some of Stokes' clearest statements not just on carving and modelling but on the general need for a dialectical approach to analysing art, especially when we take into account *experience* of art, for both artist and viewer. The focus is on "lines of equivalence", or as Bion would put it, the "caesura" or linkages between vertices or viewpoints, such as classical-romantic, and internal-external realities – the place where contraries meet and a new dimension opens out. The concept of identity in difference allows for the carving potential of colour. Stokes' ultimate formulation of "the invitation in art", in which the "enveloping pull" makes the object's otherness "more poignantly grasped", is probably his nearest approach to establishing a theory of aesthetic experience.

Chapter Four, "Mother art", documents Stokes' homage to architecture and the architectural arts as the fount and origin of his own personality development – the source of his discovery that behind all other perceptions lay the idea of the mother's body; architecture is both mother of the arts and the route by means of which art-as-mother becomes manifest. As Stephen

Kite has written, in Stokes' "architectonic" sensibility, this fluid area of response is one in which "The wall plane becomes the zone of personal encounter between our inner feelings and their outer transposition" (Kite, 2008, p. 2). The architectural qualities of nature, emerging over time, find an answering response in man's agricultural and landscape-shaping endeavours; the sustaining of life and creating a harmonious worked environment are a single concern not separate matters. These extracts make Stokes' innate congruence with Kleinian thinking abundantly clear.

Chapter Five, "Close looking", shows Stokes' principles in action as he "works-out" the symbolic congruence between his experience and that of the artist, whose inner investigations take the form not of didacticism but of "deep-laid symbol". It is the equivalent of "close reading" in literary criticism which pays minute attention to poetic diction and the sensuous impact of deep grammar. In each case the critic or aesthete is not concerned with proving a point but is engaged on a journey of discovery, "following in the steps of the Author" as Keats put it. The description of Piero della Francesca demonstrates painting-as-carving through a "chromatic sense of form" and a sense of "the family of things"; Giorgione's mysterious *Tempesta* shows the "principle of interchange" lying behind the aesthetic conflict between calm and storm; Turner's development defines the quest for "beneficence in space", the ultimate architectural achievement in painting. This last is a supreme example of aesthetic conflict successfully resolved, since it shows the author tackling his established hatreds or aesthetic dis-taste, seeking for the classical within the romantic, sticking to the disturbing line of equivalence, and working the "diaphragm" into a "receiving-screen" (Bion): that is, converting hate into love – a theme with which Stokes is much preoccupied, and here presents not just theoretically but practically.

Chapter Six, "Construction of the good mother", includes a large part of the autobiographical sketch *Inside Out* in which Stokes with hindsight reviews his preconception of

"Mediterranean" values and their ultimate conceptualization. His life's quest for the aesthetic in all things could be said to have begun with his child's wail that so mystified the adults: "I want it all right!" As Carrier has pointed out, it was after composing this "self-constructed myth" of his childhood (a continuation of his self-analysis) that Stokes was able to tackle his ambivalence towards the "modelling" modes of art he had previously marginalized.

I have included in this chapter the "Envoi" from *Venice: An Aspect of Art* which, as a statement of his principles, could really apply to all Stokes' writings.

Two tributes by personal friends (Donald Meltzer and Eric Rhode), written shortly after Stokes' death, are reprinted as appendices.

In this edition I have omitted longer footnotes, amplified some references, and occasionally made minor changes to punctuation. Where possible, references have been given both to the original editions and to the three-volume *Critical Writings* edited by Lawrence Gowing.

The painting reproduced on the book cover, *West Penwith Moor*, dates from the end of Stokes' analysis, and testifies to his affection for Cornwall where, he said, he experienced "a sense of home".

CHAPTER ONE

The quest for sanity

One day men will learn to think of sanity as an aesthetic achievement.

("Living in Ticino", 1964)

The arts of life [i]

While I might welcome the accusation of being continuously in touch with the quality of psychoanalytic thought, I should find it uncomfortable were my abstractions or my method laid at the door of that science; if only because I bring non-clinical material to bear: and again, the use I have made of my own experience is effected with little particularization except in the outside world. But more than that: the kind of mirroring I attempt is unconnected with a scientific procedure; is undivorced from an even longer preoccupation with the arts.

I do not find that these two angles of focus for existence are at variance. From the angle of the arts of life, it is at first disquieting

---

i From the foreword, *Smooth and Rough*, 1951, pp. 11-12; *Critical Writings* II, pp. 215-216.

to concede paramount importance to the issue from the balancing of forces present in infancy: and whereas the intricacy of
adulthood serves portraiture, the hardly less intricate, though
less various, finesse of the infantile state can never be enough
individualized. Hence, to explain psychologically, to "explain"
the adult in terms of the infant, seems (for an aesthetic purpose)
to be overweighted, dismissive, stultifying. A noisy weapon has
been put in the hands of the trite disputant.

Doubtless a novel lack of deceptiveness is now needed from
the man who would comprehend himself; but not humiliation,
if the probe which he himself provides but cannot point, goes
far enough. On the other hand, this deeper comprehension,
contrary to popular belief, induces a deeper awe of those vital
recapitulations embodied by conscious activity and culture.
Life, it is perhaps more clearly realized, embraces a thousand
necessary arts. I adjudge, therefore, that psychoanalytic knowledge provides firm basis, the ultimate basis, for the attitudes of
humanism.

The power to communicate [ii]

M any analogies to life are from the arts; the processes
of art condense the processes of all activity. Art is
prompt to take the place of ritual, a form that is
sometimes almost equally innocent of urgency; a form that is a
parable of urgency so far as life resembles a ritual whose early
causes and development have been forgotten and would hardly
be deduced from the ceremonies enacted.

The general character of the unconscious, especially the
many degrees of transparency to opaqueness, the incorporating
processes which breed its population, the repression thither of
much guilt, anxiety and love as well as hate, is misconstrued
by literary amateurs as the cave-like repository, sombre or wild,
of the exceptional, the far-fetched, the magical and the weird.

---

ii From "The sense of loss (2)", *Smooth and Rough*, 1951, pp. 48-51; *Critical
Writings* II, pp. 237-239.

But, on the contrary, it is consciousness that is unique and individualized; being the distorting, reflecting skin; unique the pulsating surface by which emotion is confronted with the necessitous planes of actuality, with the full radiance of reason. We shall, before long, better love ourselves again as sapient beings, with more stability than heretofore. Instead of visualizing conscious life (forgetting the to-and-fro of memory) to be a thin, ramshackle deck (removable in one piece), planted on top of romantic wildness in the holds, having some knowledge of the ingenious poetry of the ways and means, we shall marvel at and reverence a huge structure above ground, storey upon storey of amplification, of development, of repetition in accordance with the foundation and lie of the land.

The power to receive communication and to communicate is the essence of sanity. Just as infants the world over make similar noises, the preliminaries to speech, just as these sounds are common basis for the diversity of words, of intonation and of languages, so, the emotional pressures upon infancy are transformed by adult intelligence, culture, civilization, as they create therefrom poetry and prose. The individual life of love and hate, of hating of hate and loving of love – sometimes reversed – to dire, dull and amiable outcomes alike, attempts stability, a governing pattern.

Normality, differently conceived by varying societies, has been admired less for beauty of structure than for use. The happy, harmonious man, often envied by artists, was rarely himself the aesthete. Normality of the future, if it will be more nearly ideal, will have eschewed not only individual but mass neuroses. In grasping the actual, however, an entanglement with emotional life supervenes: such will be the version, with an aesthetic tinge, of "appearance" and the "thing in itself".

Truth may one day be found to possess the resolute features of the masks and covers of illusion. Except, notably, in the case of those subject to political religions, mass illusion does not, perhaps, thrive in Europe today as heretofore. We have witnessed so much put to the test: issues have been presented that must be out of scale with the potential response. We have witnessed ultimate savagery and nihilism and the limits of every hope dramatically presented. One steadfast thing, one small possession, never so accurate nor so widely diffused, is the time of day. The pips of the wireless are the voice of a father whose justice is not doubted, to whom all the little clocks and watches without hesitation repair for guidance and, if need be, for correction.

[. . .]

The riches of love flow from the religious perception of a loved object assimilated within. This source for power and stability, this balance in the face of each ancient sorrow, deprivation and aggression, cannot be disenthroned altogether, if the prime guilt and anxiety do not overpower it. Unassailable love harboured within us is full security, as all the world recognizes.

There is a keen edge to unfading division in the mind. The usual result, however, the more general result, is shallowness, the violence of shallow waters in answer to a moderate wind. Each man fights to be stable: few can dispense altogether with manic defences since they are often the means of considerable stability – at the cost, perhaps, of compulsiveness, maniacal stupidity, insensitiveness and worse.

There is only the gradual, cumulative way of no uncertainty to improve the lot, liberate the love, employ in constructiveness the needed, inevitable aggression of mankind: by the relieving of persecutory and depressive anxiety itself as well as of much of the circumstances that feed it . . . Together with our death the gift of love is all, from beginning to the end.

Relating to the object (with Donald Meltzer) [iii]

Meltzer: The essence of the transition [between the paranoid–schizoid and depressive positions] is twofold: on the one hand there is the struggle towards integration of self and objects, especially internal objects, wherein splitting and

---

iii   From "Concerning the social basis of art" (a dialogue with Donald Meltzer), in *Painting and the Inner World*, 1963, pp. 22-26; *Critical Writings* III, pp. 220-223.

exclusively part-object relations are overcome in favour of integration of the self and of whole-object relations characterized by the separate and self-contained qualities imputed to objects. The transition requires as well a shift in values from the preoccupation with comfort, gratification and omnipotence characteristic of the paranoid–schizoid organization, to the central theme of concern for the safety and freedom of the good objects, particularly again, internal ones, and especially the mother, her breasts, her babies and her relationship to the father.

While this shift in value systems has a link with Freud's distinction of primary and secondary process in mental functioning, it is by no means synonymous with it. Another item of importance, however, presents an identity of concept, though the form is expanded. Freud's categories of anxiety and guilt find expression in Kleinian theory with the conception of the two spectra of mental pain: the persecutory anxieties of the paranoid–schizoid position and the depressive anxieties such as guilt, shame, remorse, longing etc.

Now you will recall that in conversation, talking about your concept of a minimum object, we found ourselves involved in a discussion that turned out to be an investigation of the difference between what might be called "safety" in one's internal relationships as against "security". I put forward to you something that I think is inherent in Mrs Klein's work. There is no such thing as safety in object relationships to be found in the quality of the object itself. In contrast to processes characteristic of the schizoid position in which idealization, for instance, attempts to remove the object from the realm of interpersonal processes, subject to envy and jealousy, or where the splitting mechanisms attempt to reduce an object to a point where the impulse to attack it and fragment it further, is diminished; in contrast to these mechanisms of the paranoid–schizoid position, the very heart of the depressive position is the realization that security can only be achieved through responsibility. Responsibility entails integration, that is, accepting responsibility for psychical reality, for the impulsivity and affects and attitudes, for all the different parts of the self *vis-à-vis* internal and external objects. Inherent in the concept of the depressive position is the realization that the drive towards integration is experienced as love for an object, that is, as the experience of cherishing the welfare of an object above one's own comfort. It is also implicit in these theories that, for an object to be loved, it must be unique and it must have qualities of beauty and goodness which are able to evoke in the self the feelings of love and devotion. The corresponding inner object that undergoes a development parallel with the self's integration achieves those qualities as it becomes fully human in complexity. Thus it demands a life of its own, freedom, liberty of action, and the right of growth and development. In relation to such an object the feeling of love arises; the impulse, the desire, is aroused to take responsibility for all those parts of the self that are antagonistic and dangerous to the object. In essence this is the basis of the drive towards integration, towards the integrating of the various parts of the self. It perhaps is also important to mention that love for the truth becomes very strongly allied to the capacities to appreciate the beauty and the goodness of the object, since manic defences, and through them the danger of regression to the paranoid–schizoid position, have their foundations in an attack on the truth.

I think that, in so far as the creative process is an entirely private one, we have learned from Dr Segal and yourself that we should think of the artist to be representing in his art work, as through his dreams, the continuous process of the relation-ships to his internal objects, including all the vicissitudes of attack and reparation. But if we say that the artist performs acts of reparation through his creativity we must recognize that in the creative process itself, phases of attack and phases of reparation exist in some sort of rhythmical relationship. This implies that the artist, at any one moment of time in the creative process finds his objects to be in a certain state of integration or fragmentation; he consequently experiences a relative state of integration or fragmentation within the infan-tile components of his ego in relation to his objects. It must be recognized that this process necessarily involves great anxiety.

In referring to anxiety we must remember that we have in mind the whole range of persecutory and depressive anxieties.

Stokes: You are going on to speak of the role of projective identification in regard to art. Before you begin, I would like to comment on what you have said about the plain projective character. My paper, the context for this discussion,[iv] is concerned with the ordinary projection of inner objects (though I had something to say as well about the strong projection into us of haunting shapes). You accepted it as our point of departure for this discussion, with one important exception, in the matter of what I called "a minimum object", a phrase by which I drew attention to the bare, generalized, sometimes almost geometric, and in general, ideal, plane on which much artwork takes place. In the interests of the fight for integration, characteristic of the depressive position, about which, in accordance with Hanna Segal's formulation, we entirely agree that it provides the *mise-en-scène* for aesthetic creation, you object strongly to a mechanism in art, as seen by me, that forges safety for the object. You have just said, very notably: "There is no such thing as safety in object relationships to be found in the quality of the object itself [. . .]." I am very far from wanting to quarrel with that statement, as you know. But you have gone on to say that art mirrors the struggle for integration and for an integrated object; and that there are alternations of integrated and unintegrated states in the very process of making art. No one can doubt for a moment that a trend towards idealization characterizes much of the greatest art (nor the aggressive projections against which idealization is one defence). I think that a large part of the reassurance provided by art exists in the service won from paranoid–schizoid mechanisms – the transition is never complete, you have said – for what is, overall, a triumph of integration on the depressive level. Even in the best integrated people, something, at least, of the earlier mechanisms remains active, in satisfactions as well as in the conflicts. Indeed the primitive identifications, with an oral basis, that tie society, are always

---

iv "Painting and the inner world"; see extracts below (Chapters 2, 3).

particularly to the fore. The fact that you are going on to speak of the relevance to art of the primitive mechanism of projective identification among others, makes me chary of cutting any ground from under foot in the matter of early mechanisms and the production of art. Now, in *Envy and Gratitude* Melanie Klein wrote that it is not always possible to distinguish absolutely between the good and the idealized breast. Someone has said that art brings together the real and the perfect. This is not primarily a question of sugaring the pill of reality as Freud, I think, suggested the role of form to be in clothing the artist's day-dream, since to this element of invitation as he saw it, we attribute a far more fundamental part in the chemistry of the pill. All the same, art can easily be debased into a sugar-coated product that usually has great popularity among those who are hostile to art for whatever reason.

Meltzer: I think Mrs Klein was stressing the fact that only by knowing the genesis of an object can we be certain of its value.

Inner truth and outer space [v]

This wide concatenation of the outside world is more aesthetic, less passive, than those refreshing moments in which we are primarily astounded by the powerful extent of Nature; in watching a sunset, perhaps, or the fury of the sea upon rocks, or the action of submerged rocks, free to the air between waves, for ever and for ever in that brief moment throwing off the maximum water before the return of the wave. Through all the sensations of vastness and of superhuman force and rhythm which such a scene gives to the senses, surely we attend a parable of inner economy, of those forces within, seemingly foreign to us. We are looking on Nature, but at the same time we look on a clearer distribution of forces within ourselves, a clearer interaction, one more Homeric, more in style and therefore more disinterested than

---

v From *Inside Out*, 1947; *Critical Writings* II, 161-166.

is the case. We would that inner conflict were thus wind-swept, that visitation of the deeper caverns of the mind were subject to such causes as those that govern tides. And indeed they are, though it would take each of us all our years to trace such tidal movements in emotion, such governance by the few essentials. In terms of strength and space and necessity and freedom, a mental no less than a physical reminder bestows for us stark grandeur in the scene. We belong to this immense cradle of life.

In life we substitute, we repeat, we magnify, we complicate, we substitute, we repeat until the whole world is subsumed under our consciousness (childhood's world was smaller). In the course of life we embrace more and more the character of the outside world, giving ourselves to it, taking it within. At death, we and it are indistinguishable.

The more obvious process of living is a giving forth rather than a taking in. Living is ceaseless expression; ceaseless substitution, the putting of one thing into many forms both of action and of thought; the infinite ramification of a few themes. And so, in the more profound contemplation of our lot, we may look upon the truth within in terms of an outside ramification, the exquisite arrangement of space.

And Art? It will already be obvious that it is here regarded as the epitome of this central process.

We have our ways and means of keeping things alive: we forget nothing; and the deeper sources of our feeling are tapped by our environment, by material objects as well as by the human objects with whom we repeat original relationships. The external world is the instigator of memory: the external world reflects every facet of the past: it is the past rolled into the present. Projection, then, continuous and various projection, is the distinguishing characteristic of man. Animus (of how many kinds, infinite in gradation) impinges upon every look, every remark, every unspoken and spoken thought. Above all, as we regard what is external, ourselves speak there.

[. . .]

To paint a picture is metaphorically to take things to pieces in the outside world and to put them together again; a re-enactment of an early state, since the child is bent upon just such a putting together of what in fantasy he has destroyed, bitten or torn to shreds. It is likely that this element of reparation underlies all forms of art-making as well as other kinds of "constructive" activity. Historically speaking, the most usual manner in painting of reconstituting an object has been to create an image of the object, to recreate the object in terms of an essence rather than of a literal appearance. This is the manner of all conceptual art. A further development, in European art especially, has been to reconstitute the image more directly in terms of appearance, even of the momentary appearance due to a particular light. This is perhaps the more adult mode of organization, a greater adventure for the creative faculty in which it may well be lost; just as artistry is so often lost by children as they grow up and attempt in their drawing a greater fidelity to appearance. In the worst traditions of naturalistic painting, the image-making nexus, essential to any work of art, is entirely, or almost entirely, lost. For, such painting entertains a preconceived image of the appearance, involves a tricky, shoddy treatment of appearance without an image except the one which is conventional, everyday, inartistic.

The image of sanity [vi]

Formal arrangements can sometimes transmit a durable image. That is not merely to say that they are expressive. There is a sense in which every object of the outside world is expressive since we tend to endow natural things, any piece of the environment, with our associations to it, thereby constructing an identity additional to the one generally recognized. At heightened moments anything can gain the aura of a personage. But in art it should not be we

---

vi   From "The image in form", *Reflections on the Nude*, 1967, pp. 48-51; *Critical Writings* III, pp. 331-334.

who do all the imaginative work in this way. The better we understand art the less of the content we impose, the more becomes communicated. In adopting an aesthetic viewpoint – this, indeed, is a necessary contribution on our part – which we have learned from studying many works of art, we discover that to a considerable extent our attention is confined to the relationship of formal attributes and of their image-creating relevance to the subject matter. The work of art should be to some extent a strait-jacket in regard to the eventual images that it is most likely to induce. Obviously any mode of feeling can be communicated by art, perhaps even by abstract art. Nevertheless the personification of that message in the terms of aesthetic form constructs a simulacrum, a presence that qualifies the image of the paramount feeling expressed. That feeling takes to itself as a crowning attribute more general images of experience. Form, then, ultimately constructs an image or figure of which, in art, the expression of particular feeling avails itself. A simple instance lies with Bonnard, with the shape of hats in his time that approximated to the shape of the head and indeed of the breast. He seems to co-ordinate experience largely through an unenvious and loving attitude to this form. He is equally interested in a concave rounded shape. Again, when we know well an artist and his work we may feel that among the characteristic forms he makes some at least are tied to an image of his own physique or of a personal aspect in his physical responses. This also would be an instance of form as an agent which, through the means of the artist's personality as an evident first step in substantiation, allows him to construct from psychical and emotional as well as physical concatenations a thing that we tend to read as we read a face. A face records more experience than its attention at the moment we look at it.

Perhaps all we demand of a work of art is that it should be as a face in this sense. But form in the widest sense of all, as the attempted organization that rules every experience, must obviously give rise to a strong and compelling imagery so generalized that it can hardly be absent from a consciousness in working order though ordinarily present in nothing like the aesthetic strength, since were it otherwise refreshment and encouragement that we gain from art would not be necessary. Form must possess the character of a compelling apparition, and it is easy to realize that it is the icon of co-ordination.

Integration or co-ordination of what? it will be asked. Some aspect, I have argued elsewhere, of the integration of experience, of the self, with which is bound up the integrity of other people and of other things as separate, even though the artist has identified an aspect of himself with the object, has transfixed the object with his own compulsion, though not to the extent of utterly overpowering its otherness. These perceptions of relationship that are the basis of a minimum sanity demand reinforcement. Outwardness, a physical or concrete adaptation of relationship, spells out enlargement, means certainty.

It must appear a strange suggestion that art is in any way bent upon constructing an image for sanity, however minimal, in view of the wild unbalanced strains of feeling that have so often been inseparably employed in making this image. But surely if art allows not only the extremity of expressiveness but the most conclusive mode, if it constructs of expressive ness an enduring thing, that mode must incorporate an element to transcend or ennoble a particular expressiveness of which otherwise we should soon tire. We are encouraged to experience a many-sided apprehension in art. Expressiveness – it may be infantile – becomes valuable in evolving the mature embrace by form.

In the case of abstract art we are sometimes told by the artist – and it is very understandable – that we entirely mistake his work if we insist it expresses this or that. It is itself, the artist says, it does not stand for, it does not express, anything: it is not meant to suggest associations. I think he is right in the sense he means it. He is providing us, however, in his work with an experience of spatial relationships. Now it is obvious that no experience is entirely isolated, or else it is traumatic. The experience communicated by the abstract artist, on the contrary, invites comparison with other experiences and, to some extent certainly, will point to common ground with a particular aspect of visual experience in the first place or of the relationship between experiences. Abstract art would otherwise be virtually meaningless. Hence we have here an amalgam of meaning conveyed by material that transmits an image not only optical but for the mind or memory as well; unique for the eye but generalized for the mind. Here too the form constrains us to an image, and it is not merely one of our choosing.

Aesthetic experience can be defined as the opposite, indeed often as a palliative, of traumatic experience. But I am not going to try to probe the conditions of being of which this aspect of form is the symbol. I have attempted this elsewhere, as I have said. Some of the preliminaries are straightforward – for instance, the connection with the body-image. I shall partly be confining myself to this aspect.

I have often before referred to the rough-and-smooth values in building, in architecture, that are carried over into the other visual arts and, indeed, into the textures, as we have to call them, of concerted sound. Why otherwise are we forced to speak of texture to describe appositions of instrumental sound? In truth, we cannot but speak of the surface of any work of art, and equally of shape and volume, of the articulated body, metaphors by which we assert the dynamic effect of its impression and the self-completeness. Formal values vivify such images; the inevitable metaphors derive from inevitable images that accompany our apprehension of the formal qualities. In the fifteenth century courtyard of the palace at Urbino designed by Luciano Laurana, in my opinion one of the greatest masterpieces of architecture, we surely see the same thing, a justice and fairness in the smoothness of the pilasters on the brick wall. The strength of this wall is measured by the eloquence of its apertures and by the open arcade beneath. Each plain yet costly member of this building has the value of a limb: in the co-ordination of the contrasting materials there is equal care for each; together they make stillness that, as it were, breathes.

Form and wholeness [vii]

The work of art, then, because it is expressively self-subsistent, should invoke in us some such idea as the one of "entity". It is as if the various emotions had been rounded like a stone. We compare occasionally a many-sided yet harmonious personality to a work of art: the comparison suggests the notion of a psyche for once so integrated, that in contemplating it we experience the kind of pleasure we have in a well-proportioned object, and the uniformity of its surrounding space. But together with the sense of a clear totality, of an individual yet varied object (one among many), the notion, it must be remarked, contains a reference to a non-differential medium (space) which embraces the whole visible world. Now, an impression occupies real salience for an artist when it suggests an entire and separate unity, though, at the same time, it seems to be joined to the heart of other, diverse, experiences, to possess with them a pulse in common: that is the feeling the artist strives to re-create. Thus, a good poem has the closed air of an entity, of something compact that makes a dent, but its poetry is a contagion that spreads and spreads. We can always discover from aesthetic experience that sense of homogeneity or fusion combined, in differing proportions, with the sense of object-otherness.

As well as the vivid impress of self-contained totalities, we renew at the instance of aesthetic sensation the "oceanic" feeling, upheld by some of the qualities of id "language", such as interchangeability, from which poetic identifications flow.

Because it combines the sense of fusion with the sense of object otherness, we might say that art is an emblem of the state of being in love: this seems true if we emphasize the infantile introjections and reparative attitudes that are strengthened by that state. These attitudes are the fount of Form. When the artist joins them in the creative process, infantile psychic tensions concerning sense-data renew in him some freshness of vision,

---

vii   From "Form in art", *A Game That Must Be Lost* (Stokes, 1973), ed. E. Rhode, pp. 109-115.

some ability to meet, as if for the first time, the phenomenal world and the emotion it carries.

The sublimation is highly wrought. Art is, of course, a cultural activity: the "good" imagos at the back of Form are identified with the actualities or potentialities of a particular culture: indeed, the artist, "child of his age", is limited by the parent culture he serves, whose immediate yet deeper moods he portrays, as well as his own, however isolated he may be. He labours also with artistic tradition and convention, whether to swell their fruit or whether, upon desiccation, to recombine the stock.

[. . .]

In art an all-embracing element, the stage, silence, the blank canvas, can serve as the sleep of which dreams, though wakeful and rapid, are the guardians. I shall identify the interchange between an all-embracing and particularized element (thus antithetical but blended) with "good" imagos that are the bases of Form.

Form bestows not only pattern but completeness, not only the sense of separate life, but the sense of fusion. In art, repose will in some manner encompass energy. This point is crucial. Whatever the rhythm, the force, the fierceness, the furor, there is yet calm, for there is also completeness. An identity has been established amid the manifold to whose differences full value is given: just as a mirror's surface makes more comprehensive the turbulent scene reflected there. [. . .]

Form has a content of its own [. . .]. Form in art is content conceived in terms of a medium and of a culture that have been profoundly associated by the artist with the imagos described above, or with their prime surrogates.

Contemplative states [viii]

It is surely gratuitous to invoke art should the experiences of a scientist contemplating his children, his garden, a landscape, have been enough. His thoughts before the landscape are by no means circumscribed with considerations

---

viii   From "Primary process, thinking, and art", *A Game That Must Be Lost*, (A. Stokes, 1973), ed. E. Rhode, pp. 116-131.

of strata or density of the population. The shapes at which he looks, whatever the object of his immediate attention, are bound to encounter the inner landscape. I have not in mind here the perception of a phallic symbol, say, in a tree, but the impingement of the total configuration as a symbol, an aspect of symbolization *vis-à-vis* the outside world at large to which psycho-analysts are not inclined to pay prolonged attention even when attending to matters of art; whereas it has long seemed to me that this is the first, most general, sublimated content that should be held in mind in matters of art: not, it is true, from the point of view of the analysis of the artist since it is held in common, but for the understanding of art – a subject on which so many analysts have exercised themselves – and, indeed, through art, for the contemplation of the contemplative element in most experiences.

In my view, to treat of art in terms of primary process activity in the more crude sense, tied on to conscious secondary elaborations, obtains few results for the understanding of art: and the drawn-out analogies with dreams are frequently unfortunate. By and large, unlike dreams, art is a cultural activity of communication; to discuss the cultured role in terms of secondary imposition only is misleading. For one thing, what is so entirely secondary about cultural aims, ideals, characters; that is to say, how can they themselves be separated neatly from art as an embodiment of the inner life? The projection of private phantasy into that broader context of course entails mitigation or adjustment of phantasy in some respects; it also multiplies the phantasies, finds for them many analogies, elaborates the ways of condensation. Art is not a thumb that sticks out from our immense reasonableness. On the contrary, it is witness to our unceasing concern, whatever the reasonableness of which we are capable, with inner life; and so is culture.

I had thought of calling this paper "Identity in difference", a phrase that forty years ago I used frequently in descriptions of aesthetic functioning, in order to emphasize the demarcation of pictorial forms that entailed nevertheless echoes of adjacent forms so that a brotherly relationship existed; or I was referring to a unity or balance or composition wherein this close relationship sprang from the over-determination of some key segment, some shape, or from the healing progressions that belong to a fine use of chromatic differentiations with their intensity adjusted to an equality in terms of their areas. It occurs to me that the phrase "identity in difference" might be used also to describe succinctly the result of an act of projective identification, a mechanism on which, in a proper and restricted use, much of our power of recognition and first learning depended, some general forms of our participation with the world. Projective identification exemplifies both condensation and displacement.

On the subject of aesthetic value, added to pronounced self-sufficiency, I often wrote of an inviting, no less characteristic of aesthetic form, an inviting to merge with the presentation, a semiunion I described as a predominantly part-object relationship. I have not felt the need to take this back when I have stated a similar equation between the inner and outer world to be characteristic of all contemplative states. But I would today emphasize the participation of the projective-identification drive whereby the inner life and the outer object, possibly on the model of the mouth–breast part-object relationship, become pleasurably, if only because closely, associated in what has sometimes been called, for its sentimental off-shoots, "the pathetic fallacy". The fact is that we never cease to inhabit the outside world as such with our feelings. And so the simplest definition of art is that it is activity designed, by means of materials and sounds, to take advantage of, and thereby provide, an informative context for our projective inclinations, first of all, of course, those of the artist.

I shall need at this point to hazard a speculation on the nature of rationality which I take to be a fine distillation from the inner world under pressure from the external world: whereas it is commonly assumed that reality, truth, or, if you like, the laws of nature, and the logical means by which they are revealed, possess their validity independently of the mind's other drives, even though it is obvious that rationality entails constant rejection of the irrational in the way that sanity is the resolution, as well as the rejection, of what is then conceived to be the confusion of insanity, a transition we sometimes call the emergence from the predominantly paranoid–schizoid into the depressive position. It is neither here nor there that our use of the instrument of reason, as every one will agree, is constantly employed in the service of irrationality, or that in many societies, and in the case of many individuals, rationality is not far developed. The question is whether reason itself, as a process, is shorn away from the rest of the mind. Are we right to regard truth as a sophisticated notion, root as well as branch? The rare and precious search for truth for its own sake is surely an activity that cannot be isolated from an un-envious recognition of the goodness and independence of the good object, even though this recognition at the same time be denied in the inner world from which it is projected.

The commoner assumption seems to be that necessity impinging on the mind, outer rather than inner necessity, somehow inspires rational thinking to the advancement of our condition in a hostile world. The reality principle takes over. The question is, though, what is there to take over? Our first learning was not of the rational kind. We are not inclined in the psychoanalytic context to believe that any process becomes entirely divorced from the method and content of its origin. May it not be possible to detect rudiments of a causal mode of envisagement in the experiences wherein I project something that consequently comes back into me: an eye for an eye? I suggest that the roots of causality are nurtured in projection and introjection: maybe extreme emotions such as the very excessive persecutory anxiety that Bion has called "nameless dread", and Meltzer "terror", have contributed to a concept of the inevitable and necessitous, to the very iron of logic. But if the relationship be regarded as close between rationality and processes, particularly the processes predominant in early times, of the mind as a whole, it will foremost lie in the use of concepts that are the indispensable counters for the activities of reason. Most concepts are rarely clear beyond a narrow context, as if they had been imagos that now can be named but not envisaged unless particularized or embodied; by art for instance. In a delirious, romantic talk about primary process where it serves as a magical *deus ex machina* for explaining aesthetic super-dynamism, perhaps the great mistake is the implication that basic inner life lacks the element of concept and structure-that the secondary process provides all the structure.

I hope to make out a relevance in turning to Money-Kyrle's recent paper which I have found extremely impressive, "Cognitive development" (Money-Kyrle, 1968). I cannot summarize his close argument and I must take the risk that I mislead by the abstraction of a few sentences. The acquiring of knowledge, he says, "consists, not in being aware of sensory-emotional experience but in recognizing what it is." He considers first recognition to be recognition of something as a member of a class in accordance with innate preconception. "A memory image of the first member to be recognized" – he singles out the breast and the mouth – "acts as a kind of name for the class." Already in this paper Money-Kyrle has called attention to the age-old problem of universals. He persists with the notion of innate preconception because it offers the only explanation of the phenomena he envisages. I wonder whether we here see the embryo for the later aptitude to generalize and so, in the formation of concepts, for abstraction. "A class represented by a memory image is a concept", he writes. "From these two concepts" – the mouth and the breast –

> . . . it would seem that all or almost all, of the vast number of concepts we employ are ultimately derived by processes of division and combination (splitting and integration) . . . Moreover, I have the strong impression that the next steps in the construction of a set of basic concepts does not depend solely on external experience, but is itself innately predetermined. The original innate preconception of the good and bad breast or nipple seems itself to undergo a spontaneous differentiation and to budoff, as it were, other innate preconceptions – in particular, those of a good and a bad penis. If so, the mouth concept is correspondingly differentiated into mouth and vagina. Or it may be that a mouth preconception differentiates into preconceptions of mouth and vagina, and precipitates a corresponding

differentiation in the nipple concept. The exact procedure must be extraordinarily complex; but the experience of seeing a patient, who has failed to achieve such differentiations in infancy, begin to make them in dreams occurring in analysis – penis differentiating from nipple, vagina from mouth and anus, and so on – has convinced me that what I am trying to describe does, in some form, normally take place in the first few months of postnatal life. (Money-Kyrle, 1968 [1978, pp. 419-420])

Particularly notice here a power of differentiation held to be prior to displacement and condensation: a differentiation that, of course, comes into play long before the reality principle compels it: the reality principle, that is, taken to refer, as it was meant to do, to the external pressures upon instinct, not as well to an internal propensity subject to opposing mental tendencies. Now, visual perception in particular soon involves a sorting out, a grasping, of relevant differentiation; for instance, figure from ground, initiated in the first few months. We might view the early need to differentiate, in however small an area, as a necessary brake on the otherwise universal lability of substitutions and as an antecedent of a component for the later power of rational judgement. Money-Kyrle remarks the internal necessity of early differentiations to mental health, for lack of which much emotional misconception and confusion persist.

He has more to say about vital differentiations when later he speaks of the organism adapting itself to what he calls the "space–time system". The correct orientation

> . . . can be lost in at least three ways: the baby can get into it by total projective identification either out of envy or as an escape from a persecuting outer world; he can get oriented to the wrong base, in the sense that it is not one he really needs; or he can become confused in his orientation because his base is confused with a part of his own body. (Money-Kyrle, 1968 [1978, p. 425])

Though, torn from context, they may be found obscure, I quote these sentences since they emphasize the need for a power of differentiation in the earliest times, that is to say, for splitting. On the other hand, I suggest that one aspect of projective identification makes for synthesis, in what Bion has called the "normal" employment: "a primitive form of communication that provides a foundation on which ultimately, verbal communication depends" (see Bion, 1967, pp. 93-109).

You will perhaps have realized that my own exiguous speculations issue – a fount that is very far from proving them valid from the fashioning of "identity in difference" that I attribute to art, whereby art reveals the nerves, as it were, and the history of the mind. But, however rich – and they are pre-eminent – the aesthetic uses of metaphor or symbol, there resides in all art as the most immediate of its qualities, the stress upon a concrete mode of representation together with the ideographic and the verbal, three stages in representation to which Money-Kyrle refers. Art communicates in the first place through sensuous representations by means of what Freud called "thing-representations" which he attributed to the unconscious alone. Surely here exists both the most general and most poignant context for the irruption of the qualities attributed to the primary process in the matter of art. Even words, those secondary constructions essential for rational thinking, for communication, are used to some extent in art as if they were substances, as if they were things, as systems, that is to say, of sound complete in themselves while still exercising the verbal role of counters of communication about substances, about objects. I shall refer to this again.

But it is not only the long-held views about art, not only Money-Kyrle's paper, that have spurred the present writing. Another recent paper has also been a determinant, Professor Richard Wollheim's lecture "The mind and the mind's image of itself", remarkable not only in subtle yet lucid philosophical argument but for daring originality in the use of psychoanalytic considerations to clinch it, an argument to show that our reports of mental states "presuppose a conception of the mind itself." Now, he further concludes that it is a conception "tinged with spatiality":

> I should reckon it both proper and illuminating to say that our ordinary conception of the mind, while not that of a place, is one which, when distorted, spelt out, is the story of our life read in reverse: as such, it marks the path of a regression. (Wollheim, 1969, p. 216)

What he refers to here is "the subsumption of a stimulus under a bodily conception" which he relates to the dawn of thinking, having referred to Freud's account and also to Bion's. But he admits that the approximation of thoughts to corporeal substances, what he calls "the more extreme conception of the mind underlies, in many ways, the ordinary conception", although

> . . . ultimately, intellectual activity is inhibited rather than encouraged if the corporeal character of a thought remains emphatic. In its own terms Bion's account closely parallels Freud's when it depicts the schizophrenic as so overwhelmingly assimilating a thought to a bit of the body, a bad and persecuting bit, that the only course feasible to him is to evacuate the thought. (Wollheim, 1969, p. 214)

Wollheim remarks the extreme spatiality in the conception of mind that is involved in projective identification and the spatiality, in his view much modified or attenuated in normal growth and development, inherent in the imagos of internal objects, including, of course, the super-ego.

This paper strengthens me in my view of the strong corpo-reality–cum–spatiality that I have for a long time associated with art as a reflection of mental states and their communication. Though I have been writing of visual art I have suggested that the same quality permeates the other arts: that in poetry no less than in the dance, rhythm has corporeal reference: that the origin of most words goes back to substances and their interplay: that even the emotive impact of sound, the relationship of sound, may be described only in spatial, tactile and kinaesthetic metaphors. To what extent, I have asked, are they metaphors? Freud described in *The Interpretation of Dreams* the common "modification of dream-thoughts into pictorial form". We read in italics: "Considerations of representability is the peculiar psychical material of which dreams make use" (*S. E.* 5, p. 344). This should be referred, it seems obvious, to what he subsequently said in *The Unconscious* (*S. E.* 14) about "thing-representation" to which I have referred.

It is surely of interest that on the last page of the Standard Edition (apart from the reproduction of a short letter to *Time and Tide*) the following note by Freud figures, one of several notes on a single sheet of paper:

> August 22nd: Space may be the projection of the extension of the psychical apparatus. No other derivation is probable. Instead of Kant's a priori determinants of our psychical apparatus. Psyche is extended; knows nothing about it. (Freud, 1938; *S. E.* 23, p. 300).

In *Negation* (1925) Freud had written:

> Judging is a continuation, along lines of expediency, of the original process by which the ego took things into itself or expelled them from itself, according to the pleasure principle. The polarity of judgement appears to correspond to the opposition of the two groups of instincts which we have supposed to exist. Affirmation – as a substitute for uniting – belongs to Eros; negation – the successor to expulsion – belongs to the instinct of destruction. (Freud, *S. E.* 19, p. 239)

I do not wish to imply that I think the identification of the corporeal with thought is not madness. I regard rationality as an abstraction from the antecedents. Hence the first value of art, the pleasure, the relief, the relief in the exercise of more propensities of mind. This pleasure and relief, of course, is confined to those who can afford to make the admission. Naturally this number includes many whose compulsiveness and irrationality is pathological.

Perhaps it seems strange that we should value so highly the reflection in art of various mental facets since the pleasure can hardly be called an antiquarian interest in mental states. No. These other aspects still have great value in terms of communication and the apprehension of reality, in the company, that is, of the thin Prince Reason. And there is no other sphere, it seems, where they can mingle as successfully, without some insult to rationality. The entailed catharsis touches not only particular repressions – the aspect long stressed by psychoanalysis – it is also intellectual, that is to say, releases the mind's awareness of total mental function. The artist brings to bear his phantasies, his compulsions, ideals and culture; a mirror of the wider mind is constructed by the aesthetic mode of their communication, however subjective the communication may be. And the mind is surely a large part of reality. Some philosophers have taken it to be the whole.

Now for the last of the recent papers that seem to me to have a bearing. I am aware that in each case I may be expressing no more than my admiration of them; to their authors the connections I envisage may be inadmissible. This last paper is Dr Donald Meltzer's "The relation of words, language and image", from which I shall extract one point. He distinguishes between "the use of language as a mode of operation of projective identification – that is, for the communication of states of mind – while words are used for the transmission of information from mind to mind." He writes:

> Language, then, we are suggesting, is primarily a function of unconscious phantasy which employs projective identification as its mode of communication. The substance of its communications is states-of-mind. Its means of communication is fundamentally primitive, namely song and dance . . . What I am suggesting is that we consider "vocalization" as the symbolic form and "verbalization" as its corresponding notational system.[ix]

I would stress the physical or concrete mode of expression by means of vocalization as the basis of language throughout this

---

ix This paper was later incorporated in *Dream Life* (Meltzer, 1983), pp. 96-113.

account, thereby bringing language in line with the mode of the arts that are the offshoots of language for the communication of states of mind.

It is difficult, even when constructing a scientific presentation, to put art altogether out of court, and it doesn't seem desirable. Words can be so dead; bad, clumsy writing can be painful and distant from us, whereas the simplest statements can seize the mind, haunt the mind, if the sound and rhythm of the words are felicitous. I believe in this context that "felicitous" means assimilation to the general character of states of mind, as if we had introjected a projection that comes back to us enriched. The communication is full, becomes a participation in the mental commonality wherein corporeal imagery still plays so large a part. Moreover, the less we treat of words in our writing as the voiceless digits of a code, the closer our thought about meaning tends to be, due to this care for their effect.

Psychoanalysis discovered that every activity contains symbolic functions. We do not consider the mathematical problem to be devoid of various symbolic significations for the practitioner. Emotional need inspires the exercise of rationality though it plays no part in the process: the thinking itself is then autonomous. But the doubt remains whether rationality itself is finally distinguishable in an absolute sense from other conceptualizing proclivities.

What cost does thinking, in the strictest, most developed sense, have to pay for mind: I mean in the nature of the process, rather than in regard to emotions that have spurred, or that still direct, the thinking? Whatever the answer – and perhaps the fact should be considered in making answer – the mental achievements with most air of completeness are those of art, those strained all the time through a larger area of mind. One reason, it seems, is that not only does painting, in particular, offer artist and spectator a higher exercise in the discriminatory powers of vision but that art, in this and in other ways, revivifies, enlarges upon, the link between all mental activities and our active apprehension of outside things together with their introjection. Thus, as I have said, most language is of necessity metaphor, employs, at any rate in origin, images of objects. To be reminded by the construction in art – to be reminded of concreteness accompanying abstraction, never ceases (in spite of schizophrenic excess) to be generally appropriate, indeed corrective, whatever an enquiry may be. Thing-representation is primary, at no stage entirely eliminated. Consequently, the case of the word "primary" has lost here the contingent sense of "primary process", though it includes that reference.

[. . .]

Now, however strong the impact and demands of external necessity, they can bring little awareness of the actual, except to the mind that has a grip, though tenuous, on sanity, since sanity is an adjustment to the external world and to the external figures that is based on a modicum of respect for truth. I use the word "truth" rather than "actuality" or "reason" because the sane propensity is first an admission of psychic reality, that is to say, depends upon some acceptance, however small, of the limitation of defences. Thus, the study of psychosis has shown that the sense of reality is bound up with even a minimum degree of ungrudging and enduring admission, among other admissions, of the good as good. It might therefore be argued that it would sometimes be an advantage in the psychoanalytic context to speak of a truth, rather than a reality, principle; that the usage would help smooth presentations of the psyche in terms of those primary and secondary processes that, in the view of this paper, are much in need of tailoring at the joins. We would do better, in my opinion, to discriminate upon a one-piece process: and such, I believe, is largely the tendency of much present-day psychoanalytic thought, an undertaking that leaves untouched the distinction between conscious and unconscious.

CHAPTER TWO

Art and the inner world

Painting and the inner world [i]

It seems desirable that I give a precise account of what I mean by the inner world, the one of Freud and Melanie Klein. Apart from the fact that I claim no precise picture, there is always the difficulty that the concepts of psychoanalysis are little known and far less understood, yet it is impossible to interpolate several treatises available elsewhere.

The aspect of the psyche that most concerns our context is the potential chaos and the attempts to achieve stability whether predominantly through defences of splitting such as getting rid of parts of the psyche on to other people, or through denial, omnipotence, idealization, or whether predominantly by the less excluding method, the prerogative of the truly adult being, that entails recognition of great diversity in the psyche under the aegis of trust in a good object. The word "object" may seem obscure but it is used with determination. By means of introjection, the

---

i From *Painting and the Inner World*, 1963, pp. 5-9; *Critical Writings* III, pp. 210-213.

opposite of projection, the ego has incorporated phantasy figures (and part-figures such as the breast) both good and bad. These are objects to us not only because they have come from without but because they can retain within the psyche their phantasied corporeal character. The ego itself may be much split: many parts may have been projected permanently to inhabit other people in order to control them, an instance – it is called projective identification – of the interweaving of outer and inner relation-ships. Though this phantasy-commerce be deeply buried in our minds, it colours, nevertheless, as I have indicated, the recep-tion of sense-data in much-transposed terms. Form in art, I have urged elsewhere, reconstitutes the independent, self-sufficient, outside good object, the whole mother whom the infant should accept to be independent from himself, as well as the envel-oping good breast of the earliest phase, at the foundation of the ego, the relationship with which is of the merging kind. In this reparative act the attempt must be made to bring less pleas-ing aspects of these objects to bear, parallel with the integrative process in the ego as a whole that art mirrors no less.

Furthermore, within a pattern of integration, there intrude narrow compulsive traits both of offence and defence in sublimated forms. We are likely to observe an obsessional aspect of art within the broad compulsion to repair and to integrate what has been threatened, scattered, or destroyed. Indeed, it is a narrower compulsive element – we shall find it in Turner – that bestows on much art a quality of urgency and inevitability, causing the spectator to feel that a rigid driving force, having attained aesthetic sublimation, becomes most impressive partly because art is never to be divorced, within its limits, from truth and understanding, and partly because a successful sublimation of obsessional attitudes subject to the major conspectus, signifies that some degree of aesthetic (i.e. integrative) employment has been won from tendencies often hostile to any integrative role.

There would be nothing to art could it be exercised in despite of temperament. Not even the framework ordained by culture can be used to contrive for aesthetic expression a rule of thumb: though his working in a settled style will cloak it thickly, the artist has needed his temperament. He may work all his life within a strict convention: on the other hand, a few of the greatest European painters have manifestly rediscovered, re-allocated, more and more of themselves in the terms of their art: their discoveries and extensions of themselves have ensued directly from further aesthetic exploration. Art is built directly upon previous art, indirectly upon the artist's courage about himself and about his surroundings. The student today builds little by rote that he can subsequently dismember, enlarge, and rebuild: he attempts an unprecedented immediacy of expression: the close of an evolution is tried at the beginning. I believe the fruitfulness to be limited as a rule. This is the context for the appreciation of Turner in Part III.[ii]

To return to inner objects. There will have been many visitors to Rome and to the Vatican who will have found daring shapes insistent beside the traffic roar, mingling with the contrasted movements in a street. The painted forms from galleries survive, enter and inhabit the city. The palpable images that we saw welling out of walls and canvasses touch us profoundly because they reflect figures in ourselves, incorporated figures, whose inner presence is more variable and far less orderly. We relish it that inner tensions be transformed into the outer corporeality of contrasted attitudes amid the simulated breadth of the outside world. For a few people, at any rate, there is a related perception of dreams from which only a limited anxiety remains, a similarity with the salient impressions of shape planted in our minds by Roman sightseeing; in regard to dreams, that is, whose content we cannot at once recall. Some people may have an impression from the dream, nonetheless, of density perhaps, or of great space, or of a dominant form: in effect, of an epitome in the terms of substance and space. I call it an epitome because I have found that when this impression has become the surviving imprint, yet, when later, the dream has been recalled in some detail, the sensation of an arrangement of forms had been broken up into this recall, as if these formal elements had synthesized or

---

ii See below, Chapter 5.

resolved the contradictions of the content into something not only simple but tangible. Owing to the corporeal nature of the adult's inner objects, it seems that a dream can deposit a residue of sensations of shape, as does art, the more general, and therefore less painful, though not altogether distorted, perception of inner objects.

Much visual art is founded in accumulated designations of outer character and the world of space. This conscious aim provides transcendental dimensions for the inner world, in a concrete form. We do not usually associate the word "transcendental" with a condition expressly concrete, but it is surely admissible in the case of some methods of outer contemplation, and particularly of art that offers a single object to the senses, a version of inner objects available as one interaction. Inner idols, hated and loved, together with some of the defences or rituals they impose, are compounded. Though the subject-matter of a painting be what the theologians call carnal beauty, in so far as the picture is a work of art, the particular erotic stimulus – no painted flowers seem to have scent, no aesthetic apple cause mouths to water – becomes secondary to a more general awareness of availability that has been heightened rather than dominated by the manifest erotic content. But it is understandable to mistake or to resist the point of art, to find in its scentless flowers no suggestion but of their deadness, at any rate when naturalistic art has been considered as the only norm.

It follows from what has already been said that the inner world encountered under the aegis of aesthetic form, elicits relationships to the basic good objects, namely the self-subsistent mother and the enveloping good breast or part-object. Just as an integrated psyche reads and tempers experience by the light of a firm trust in the relationship to these good objects, so the manifold expressiveness of art, in virtue of its form, figures within their orbit; the wider the expressiveness the better, as a rule, inasmuch as aesthetic form obtains significance from the varied material to be unified of the artist's temperament, of his culture and of his inheritance from art, as well as from his subject-matter. We spectators, prepared to view the modern work of art as a good object, may contemplate in this manner an aspect of our own culture that is anything but good, yet we would not need recourse to denial or to other defence. As is well known, the artist is both the leader and the servant of his time. He is able in some degree – only some degree – in accordance with a new cultural theme or accentuation, to lend himself to the expression of a psychical position that under other aesthetic circumstances (in accordance with other cultural circumstances) might or might not have been available to him. We can have no conviction whatsoever concerning the way that oven the greatest of artists would have worked had they lived in other periods. The artist's perspicacity about culture, about what upholds, destroys or ameliorates his society and his art, provides both a condition and an earnest of his truthful comment upon the inner world that he finds reflected while examining any outer situation. It is in line with the common disposal of feeling by means of projection, employed aesthetically for the purpose of insight in regard to both the within and the without and their relationship: otherwise the artist would achieve no integration, no art.

This brings me to the subject of bad objects, of aggression, of envy, of all that is negative. Again, these drives, and the objects imbued with them, could not figure in art – and they figure prominently – except under the sign of co-ordination, of the form in art that stems from the presence of good objects. Tragic art, to be so, must bear nobility. But many appreciators today seem to find it more exciting if formal elements can be observed barely to survive a monstrous expression of, say, greed. What is entirely negative or chaotic, or merely unfeeling, can never be art, and what is near to it is never great art.

Absorption and attention [iii]

There is a sense in which we absorb the object of our attention: we speak of absorbing or imbibing knowledge while, for the moment, the rest of the world is

iii From the epilogue, "The luxury and necessity of painting", *Three Essays on the Painting of Our Time*, 1961, pp. 20-23; *Critical Writings* III, pp. 157-160.

excluded. Except for contemplative acts we do not mentally imbibe a thing as an end in itself but as part of a wider activity. Though things and their systems remain outside us, we seem to get to know them by taking them in; for the most part, however, we do not will them to flood through every atom of our being in entering the store of what we call the mind. The work of art, on the other hand, though by definition a complete and enclosed system, strongly suggests to us physical and mental states of envelopment and of being enveloped. These identifications vary from strong manipulation of the object to an absorption of it and a sinking into it; I have used the word "envelopment" as shorthand. Since art is useless, it exists solely for the contemplative act in which the senses are not the mere vehicles; the appeal is first to them. Two important results follow: as the senses are the feelers by which we apprehend the otherness of outside things, the otherness or object-nature of the work of art is stressed in this act of its contemplation; yet, as I have said, the ruling attention is also engaged by the process of its absorption no less than by the more obvious projecting therein of our feelings.

The great work of art is surrounded by silence. It remains palpably "out there", yet none the less enwraps us; we do not so much absorb as become ourselves absorbed. This is the aspect of the relationship, held in common with mystical experience, that I want to stress, because the no less important and non mystical attitude to object-otherness in aesthetic appreciation has been better admitted. Aesthetic form immediately communicates, as well as a symbolic image of an integrated ego (Stokes, 1958), the answering image of a reconstituted and independent "good" object. This object thereupon becomes incorporated with a satisfaction that evokes in turn a more permeating ground for what is felt to be good, and so a symbol for the "good" breast. The process entails the feeling of "a pulse in common", of a heightened identification between the appraiser and his object: it is a process that has been accentuated in the so-called conventionalized or conceptual styles of the graphic arts; without ado they impart a generalized image imposed upon what is particular, upon what is mere appearance, transcendent equally of self and of object-nature. Evoking, through the creation of symbolic inducements, the manner of primitive attachment to a part-object (e.g. the breast), art has served ritual, religion, and every cultural aim.

In this context, but more particularly outside it, that is to say, in examples which lack the focus of a narrow cultural ideal, we find an employment [. . .] for a type of experience that may be called visionary, though coupled (as assuredly it must be in the creation of art) with an insistence upon the independence of a limited, self-sufficient object.

What common analogy can we find for so strong an absorption of ourselves into other things? As a matter of fact such identification is extremely common: an element of it enters into all group attitudes, all states of contemplation and physical engrossment. The most common is surely the state of sleep wherein we discern best the "oceanic feeling" as Freud called it, a loss of identity that he referred to the infant's satisfaction at the breast with which he is one, a part-object that does not suggest the distinctiveness from its perceiver of a whole object. (There are many methods of confusion with the object, under the stress of predominantly negative feelings, that result in serious loss of ego power. The affirmative quality of aesthetic value I have in mind is bound to be related, largely in a compensatory manner, with these mechanisms of attack and of defence.)

Dr Lewin's so-called "dream screen" is distinguished from the rest of the dream and defined as the blank background upon which the dream picture appears to be projected; it has

> . . . a definite meaning in itself and . . . represents the idea of "sleep"; it is the element of the dream that betokens the fulfilment of the cardinal wish to sleep, which Freud considered responsible for all dreaming. Also, it represents the maternal breast, usually flattened out, as the infant might perceive it while falling asleep. It appears to be the equivalent or the continuation, in sleep, of the breast hallucinated in certain pre-dormescent states, occasionally observed in adults. (Lewin, 1948, p. 224).

Whether or not the dream screen is well authenticated, it serves to illustrate the formal value to which I would point in aesthetic experience, usually associated with a subject-matter (the dream itself). In such projections the good breast is of an illimitable character: art is here joined by religious and philosophical yearning for the absolute, so primitive and, some will think, so destructive of good sense in a pretended context of universal truth. The superb place for it is in useless art, harnessed to an equal emphasis upon object-otherness. We must realize at the same time that more generally an oral character in experience is very common; the modes of identification necessary to culture and to cultural behaviour, in part depend upon it.

Thus, in virtue of its form at least, art rehearses favourable relationships free of excessive persecution, greed, and envy. Convention, stylization, the power to generalize, are among the means of furthering the enwrapping component in aesthetic form: where one line does the job of two, in any simplification, we experience the emphasis upon singleness. But at the same time the identical formal qualities, such as pattern, that lend themselves to an envelopment theme, are the means also for creating the object-otherness, independence, and self-containment of the work of art: it "works" on its own, "functions" in the way of an organism: this phantasy accompanies the one of our being enveloped, but is connected with another that projects the ego in terms of an integrated figure in which opposite characteristics coalesce. The idea of beauty, I have said elsewhere (Stokes, 1958), projects the integrated ego in the terms of a corporeal figure.

I add this note in regard to Dr Lewin's description of his dream screen as a flattened breast. One thinks at once of the flattened shapes especially of low relief in much art of the world, particularly Quattrocento low reliefs, often of the Mother and Child; and, more generally, one thinks of the picture plane in painting that is preserved at all costs by modern art; more generally still, one thinks of the little recessions, lines, and protuberances of pilasters, for instance, of the markings on frieze or cornice, by which architecture reconstitutes the body. I wrote many years ago: "Architecture is a solid dream for those who love it. One often wakes from sleeping without any recollection of a dream but conscious of having experienced directions and alternatives and the vague character of a weighty impress in harmony with the non-figurative assertiveness of building. In architectural experience, however, changing surfaces, in-out, smooth-rough, light-dark, up-down, all manner of trustful absorption by space, are activated further than in a dream; full cognizance of space is sign enough of being wide awake. The state of sleep has thus been won for actuality."

And so, too, I make bold to say, in art altogether.

All art is of the body [iv]

The balanced emotional estimation of the body is an ideal. One may doubt whether any human being has attained entire integration of those hidden feelings. It remains the quest, an impetus of adult search including the one of art. Indeed the contribution of art is quickly apparent; for instance in regard to the huge concern particularly of the infant and the child – a concern, therefore, that will always considerably persist – about the inside of the body, though the nearest even to an intuitive formulation at which most people arrive is in the context of hypochondria and psycho-somatic illness when these conditions have been recognized for what they are. Whereas the art of the written word is with difficulty and indirectness centred on this matter, portraits and paintings of the figure are less hard to inter-pret. Rembrandt, it seems to me, painted the female nude as the sagging repository of jewels and dirt, of fabulous babies and magical faeces despoiled yet later repaired and restored, a body often flaccid and creased yet still the desirable source of a scarred bounty: not the bounty of the perfected, stable breast housed in the temple of the integrated psyche that we possess in the rounded forms of classical art, but riches and drabness joined by the infant's interfering envy, sometimes

---

iv From "Art and embodiment", *Reflections on the Nude*, 1967, pp. 36-40; *Critical Writings* III, pp. 325-328.

with the character of an oppressive weight or listlessness left by his thefts. There supervenes, nonetheless, a noble acceptance of ambivalence in which love shines.

This is not necessarily to hint at Rembrandt's emotional equipment nor to stigmatize a bias in seventeenth-century northern European culture. On the contrary the contrasting classical conception is very rare: it is far more common to discover in art the implication with the inside of the body: we accept it that the Athenian achievement is without parallel and that the emptiness and falsity to which the Greek ideal would often be reduced (though the inspiration will never disappear) could cause it to be less accessible even to some who, like Rembrandt, studied and borrowed from classical composition, learning especially how to achieve the look of inevitability whereby to dominate the larger aspects of design.

Rembrandt constructed a stable format out of contrary emotions, from a varied human condition to which he allowed by the granular additiveness of his technique, the progression to a munificence that crowns other impressions like a gratitude that has finally overcast an envy. He has shown in sum, as Kenneth Clark said of his portraiture, "the raw material of grace", strands of negative feeling, for instance, about the body limited to the original zones, a process that will have entailed some withdrawal of those parts of the self that have been sent into the object to plunder or to command; for otherwise the affirmation that I am I and they are they, an objective of art, cannot be clearly stated.

We are intact only in so far as our objects are intact. Art of whatever kind bears witness to intact objects even when the subject-matter is disintegration. Whatever the form of transcript the original conservation or restoration is of the mother's body. And whereas pictorial art employs and stimulates those infantine phantasies – they are many – that utilize the eyes for omnipotent projections, for omniscience, it enlarges upon the reassuring endurance of objects in the shadow of this attack: they are enthroned by the artist by means of a pictorial settlement wherein they may surrender themselves only to that multiform composition which symbolizes the integrated elements of the self no less than of the other person.

[. . .]

A painting of the nude, therefore, is but one of the corporeal lessons set by art. There is a sense in which all art is of the body, particularly so in the eyes of those who accept that the painted surface and other media of art represent as a general form, which their employment particularizes, the actualities of the hidden psychic structure made up of evaluations and phantasies with corporeal content.

Weighty articulation and hazy presences [v]

The controlled tenderness of Bellini's Christian piety, as seen in *The Dead Christ Supported by Angels* (National Gallery), embraces an illumined land. That view of the body had come down to him from Attic Greece. Pentelic sanity confronts muted eloquence. The stillness of the candid dead torso dignifies life without separating it from grief. Dead, the body of Christ connects with the living who take into their minds the image of Christ as an ideal body, it is suggested here, as a chest in part, smooth, sloping, elephantine in wisdom; breathing, it seems, a warm silence. More generally we are offered images of life and death, deft angels and the mortified head of the corpse. The habit of bodies, whether sensitive or dead, is disclosed once more: we are told that in the variety of meanings to which it points a body is as expressive as a face. The partial nude always conveys the sense of disclosure: it is appropriate here to the Christian meaning. At the same time the angels perform a slow gentle wrapping of the corpse.

Many characteristics of flesh are suggested by this delineation, but only one characteristic is omni-present to which other

---

v   From "The image in form", *Reflections on the Nude*, 1967, pp. 56-58; *Critical Writings* III, pp. 337-339.

delineations are subordinate: shape against a back ground. The spaces thus contrived are roughly triangles. The angels' heads both echo and vary Christ's head, the cylinders of their arms the corpse's arms. The element of geometry or of reduplication is an armature, the aesthetic armature, to which our feelings, as if they too could be solid things, as if they could be clay, cling; that is to say our feelings of contact, our meeting with a separated object or with ourselves now encouraged to separate from the splitting of ourselves. We feel in ourselves the tautness of the angels' feathered wings, the wrinkled clinging sleeve, the arm covering in the making for the corpse below those wings. We feel in us the corpse's beautiful listless hands. Christ's right arm droops but it is half-supported by a ledge on which the fingers bend, and by the angels' enwrapping grip. That demonstration of gravity serves less the effect of momentum than of poise, so nearly compounded of compensations as to be rest.

How often is this the effect upon us of the Old Masters, particularly of paintings with nudes. In my own mind I revisit early years abroad, the sense of discovery in many galleries, the predominant effect of the pictures in relation to the discomfiture of loneliness. Art meant oasis for the body as well as for the mind but also a ritual that affirmed unalterable contact, on the whole in a fully adult sense, rescued from the excess that had obscured or depleted an embrace.

Rembrandt's *Belshazzar's Feast* in the National Gallery is far from conveying this involucre of Pentelic marble; on the contrary, it shows human beings with the incorrigible character of scored, used pots. A darker conception of the body assumes a vivid clay. Hence Belshazzar's imposing pallor even though he suggests a richly feathered hen or turkey amid a treasury of filth, though the quilted magisterial stomach mounts to a plucked neck and head. Leaden with the threads of gold and silver, turban and diadem reiterate the blindness of heaped matter as does the great weighted see-saw of Belshazzar's outstretched arms. The woman recoiling on the right who spills from a cup herself suggests a rounded, stoppered vessel. The clattering gold, like all treasure, has its threat or is threatened. Amid the fur of light upon the wall incomprehensible letters speak out the traumatic counterpart sometimes associated with these bodily products.

I believe that strong feelings of such a kind, or feelings derived from them, possessed Rembrandt; they are one root of his power; and that otherwise he could not so magnificently have imposed the weighty articulation, for instance, of Belshazzar's right hand.

Many of us find Rembrandt to be the greatest of artists, I think because no artist approaches him in projecting the feel I have spoken of, the feel of presences not only substantiated from observation in the outside world but substantiated equally from the hazy presences in the mind. We are aware of a lineage for his every face far beyond the range of iconographic study. These presences are charged, weighty, condensed from the light and from the dark literally and metaphorically, with a finer drama than the apparition of writing on a wall. They are compendia, bodies that manifest the history of their growth: each speck gives power to an opaque fellow. In a very remarkable book about Soutine, just published, Andrew Forge has written of Rembrandt in similar strain. He has this sentence: "This is his (Rembrandt's) measure, that his architecture is as ambitious as his material is earthy."

The art of appreciation [vi]

Our relationships to all objects seem to me to be describable in the terms of two extreme forms, the one a very strong identification with the object, whether projective or introjective, whereby a barrier between self and not-self is undone, the other a commerce with a self-sufficient and independent object at arm's length. In all times except the earliest weeks of life, both of these relationships, in vastly differing amalgams, are in play together, as is shown not only by psychoanalysis but by art, since the work of art is par excellence a self sufficient object as well as a configuration

---

vi From "The luxury and necessity of painting", *Three Essays on the Painting of Our Time*, 1961, pp. 10 -17: *Critical Writings* III, pp. 151 -156.

that we absorb or to which we lend ourselves as manipulators. (The first generic difference between styles lies in the varying combinations by which these two extremes are conveyed to us). Here is to be observed a fundamental connection of art with the culture from which it arises; for, art helps us both to identify ourselves with some aspect of our culture, to incorporate cultural activities or to reject them, and at the same time to contemplate them as if they were fixed and hardy objects.

From the angle of contemplation culture is art – hence, once more, the necessity of having art-since culture is most easily seen as an object for contemplation in aesthetic terms. Moreover, a cultural reconciliation of what is various, and even opposite, is perceived, when reflected in art, as a symbol for the integration that we have carried out upon contrary urges, opposite feelings, once widely separated, about one and the same person. In painting his picture the artist performs an act of integration upon the outside world that has reference, then, as well as to the independence of objects, first to the re-creation and to some resolution of his own inner processes, next in regard to the organization of the ego in a generalized sense, and finally in regard to a cultural significance. The result is an interplay between these modes of organization to the end of making one of them more poignant since it possesses the services of the others.

[. . .]

There is no hard-and-fast division between the appreciator and the creator of art. Indeed, whatever his conscious interest or knowledge, I have no doubt that the artist is potentially the most highlytrained appreciator, often confined in range of interest by the preoccupation of his own creative field. This is but to emphasize again in a different manner that art is a cultural activity though the fount be hidden and untutored. Were it otherwise, art would not mirror the whole man, the whole of his capacity.

[. . .]

Picasso is reported to have said that as a child he could draw like Raphael but that later, as an adult, it had taken him a long time to learn to draw like a child. It seems that the character of our culture has inspired an element of regression: it inspired Picasso's early appreciation of the values of negro sculpture, a very important part of his creativeness. We taste a new humility and a new arrogance, a sophistication and a barbarity in all the people and all the things surrounding us: and I do not use the word "taste" altogether metaphorically since I would stress the oral component in our attitudes to parts of our environment: as presented by art, I have said, it does not overwhelm us since, as well as in the terms of envelopment and incorporation, we are shown an aspect of our environment and "mental climate" by the painter as an enclosed object, at arm's length, reflecting what I have called two basic relationships to objects. They are usually experienced together; in art alone their collusion seems perfected to the extent that we appear to have the cake and to eat it without a greedy tearing, the object to incorporate and the object set out and self-contained. Surely the status of this cake is the one of the "good" internal object, the "good" breast which, as Melanie Klein (1957) has repeatedly said, formed and forms the ego's nucleus, the prototype not only for all our "good" objects but, in the unenvious, unspoiling relationship with it, for happiness.

But it is always a prime error to search only for derivations that are positive, affirmative. I have not pointed to the fact that part of the aesthetic compulsion will have a negative basis in the component of aggression and, perhaps, of organ deficiency as well as in the threat, perhaps always present, of incipient confusion. We know of several great painters who have had ceaseless trouble with their eyes, imaginary or real. When the trouble has been imaginary we must impute to them an unconscious sense of guilt, unusually strong, in connection with the greedy, prehensile, and controlling act of vision as it has appeared to the phantasy in early years. To observe is partly to control, to be omnipotent: whereas the exercise of the cruel power continues in the making of art, it is used also to reconstruct what thereby is dismembered: in reflecting such combined yet antithetical drives, a work of art symbolizes the broader integrating processes. The aesthetic account of integration is an end-in-itself, unlike the stock syntheses that construct a character type, professional, class, or national, often valued beyond all other ego projections by unaesthetic persons. Genius displays a new mending of impulse, of feeling, with such conviction that there issues from it a novel treatment of subject-matter as of form. Cézanne applied a steelbright knife to pattern and to distance: he introduced love and respect into an extraordinary attack upon his apples and upon the landscapes of his home. His paintings are unified by a play of glinting cuts that both bisect and glorify the contour. It is above all composers who demonstrate easily the varieties, and even the contrariety, implicit in a theme. What twists of combined feelings Mozart contrived within the clear cascade of a chamber work.

Many artists of an opposite temperament to Cézanne's will have availed themselves of his discoveries. Considered psychologically the development of art is no less complicated than the view from any other approach. But I want to stress a factor that has usually been simple, the compulsion to "get things right" issuing in part from the fear of deformity and of aggressiveness. In the case of naturalistic painting the first test of what "looks wrong" has been very simple. In drawing a jug how shameful it is that a side should become swollen or should be impoverished, how poignant and sacrilegious the lopsidedness. Many present-day artists defy this fear and scan the lopsidedness of our environment: modern art tends to conventionalize ugliness and distortion in the search for comprehensive balances: the vibrant power wanes to correct each enormity without devitalization, since art must reflect as well as affirm: idealism in art has been the face put upon some degree of truth, upon some need of balance amid discord: also the unabashed shape of the deformed jug may have this timeless quality. In the past undeformed shapes have sometimes been balanced in a picture asymmetrically: today we often see deformed shapes balanced squarely.

I have already introduced a negative approach in attributing the development of modern painting partly to the nineteenth-century vulgarization of architecture. Ugliness has strengthened not only confusion but a desire for collapse: in art we will here discern an amalgamation of negative and positive components.

A collapsed room displays many more facets than a room intact: after a bombing in the last war, we were able to look at elongated, piled-up displays of what had been exterior, mingled with what had been interior, materializations of the serene Analytic Cubism that Picasso and Braque invented before the first war; and usually, as in some of these paintings, we saw the poignant key provided by some untouched, undamaged object that had miraculously escaped. The thread of life persists, in the case of early Cubist paintings a glass, a pipe, a newspaper, a guitar whose humming now spreads beyond once-sounding walls that have become clean and tactile remains. In such strange surroundings, not altogether unlike the intact yet empty buildings invented by Chirico, the brusque accoutrements of comfort for pavement life, the one of the café, extend a great sense of calm: a simple shape and a simple need emerge from the shattering noise and changing facets of the street. Later work by Picasso is more disturbing, since he has broken off and recombined parts of the body, often adding more than one view of these partobjects. Disruption of flesh and bone extends to the vitals; but the furor of his genius is such that the sum of misplaced sections does not suggest the parts of a machine: on the contrary, in the translated bodies, as in the rent room, of Guernica, there exist both horror and pathos as well as aesthetic calm: the interior of the body is not represented as a ruined closet but as part of an exterior decor. Similarly, the New York Manager of Picasso's ballet, *Parade,* wore his ribs outside his costume and outside the child's skyscraper attached to his head. In the period known as Synthetic Cubism, Picasso and Braque had joined into whole objects upon tilted table-tops the piled-up abstract bric-a-brac accumulated in Analytic Cubism, to an enfolded effect as fresh as fruit. Strong, jagged pattern, a wrought-iron jointure, the curve of a rib blunt or acute, typify enduring characteristics in the manifold variations of Picasso's art, a giant in our times.

The distinctiveness of what we call modern art does not lie in the degree of conventionalization or of distortion or in a total neglect of appearances but in the treating by means of such methods of all experiences as if they were rudimentary; impact takes precedence of the values revealed by the last ripple on the pond. Things are already in bits and must themselves be broken up into absorbable parts. The emphasis upon strong impact is an emphasis not only upon the projection of proprioceptive or interoceptive sensations and images associated with a mere part of the body, but consequently upon the merging or incorporating function that belongs pre-eminently to our relationship with any part-object, in the first place the breast of infanthood: we cannot attribute originally to the infant an awareness of whole or separate objects either visually or imaginatively, only of highly coloured attributes or parts that in their supreme goodness or badness are assimilated with himself. In modern art, then, the wealth of adult experiences is often endowed with this primitive cast that is normally retained at such strength in adult life for some states only, such as sleep. I am here referring to a treatment in the work of art, not entirely to the effect of the work itself, which by definition brings to us also the sense of a whole and self-sufficient object. On the other hand, a unifying simplification of shape (and often a shape's mere exaggeration) to some degree figures in all plastic art: it facilitates the clutching impact, the easy identification, characteristic of relationship with a part-object, whereby the world is homogeneous. As well as to observe, Form induces us to partake.

The artist and the art appreciator (with Donald Meltzer) [vii]

Meltzer: Having now discussed projective identification in both its destructive aspect, and its constructive aspects as an instrument for communication of a primitive and concrete sort, I think we are in a position to examine the psychology of the person who views art. (Of course we are not restricting ourselves to the viewing of visual art only.) I am talking about people who view art as an important, and perhaps

---

vii From "Concerning the social basis of art" (a dialogue with Donald Meltzer), *Painting and the Inner World*, 1963, pp. 31-38; *Critical Writings* III, pp. 226-230.

even central, part of their inner-life processes. I am therefore excluding the people who view art from more peripheral motivations. It will perhaps be useful to indicate that, in so far as contemplating art is a form of intercourse between viewer and artist, it has an exact parallel in the sexual relationships between individuals. We would want to distinguish here between events in which sexual relationships are casual regarding choice of partner, being in this sense a direct extension of the masturbation process. (By this I don't mean to imply necessarily that it is an extremely harmful or sadistic matter.) In contrast, there are those events of sexual inter course in which contact with the other person's inner world is central. Here, of course, we would have to distinguish be tween acts of love and acts of sadism, again in the latter case not necessarily implying that these acts of sadism would have to be carried out in objectively perverse ways. In acts of love we know very well that processes both of projecting love and good objects, as well as of introjecting from the love-partner, are going on. In a similar way, in a destructive intercourse the projecting of bad parts of the self and of the destroyed objects, as well as the masochistic submission of one's self to this form of abuse are enacted. There is a parallel, then, in the intercourse between the artist and the viewer: the artistic production itself is a very concrete representation of what is transported. I think that the viewer we have in mind is not at all at play: while his social relationship to his companions may be part of his play life, towards art he is at work, exposing himself to a situation of intensely primitive (oral) introjection through his eyes or ears or sense of touch. That is, he enters a gallery with the aim of carrying out an infantile introjection, with the hope, in its constructive aspects, of obtaining something in the nature of a reconstructed object. Conversely, in a masochistic sense, a viewer may be going to expose himself to the experience of having projected into him a very destroyed object or a very bad part of the self of the artist. This aspect of masochism I have discussed a bit in my paper on "Tyranny".[viii]

[. . .]

---

viii   Revised in *Sexual States of Mind* (Meltzer, 1973), pp. 143-150.

Stokes: I think you could say that because an evocation of the breast relationship and of the relationship to the mother herself are built into formal presentation as a perennial basis, we are induced, far more strongly than we would otherwise be, to contemplate the detailed of the processes of the inner life that a work of art may contain.

What you have said about the oral introjection performed by the viewer points particularly to the enveloping action of a work of art and to the breast relationship from which it derives. The work of art is basically a reconstruction not only of the whole and independent object but of the part-object, the beneficent breast. I refer once more to the general, the formal, value rather than to the impact, thereby magnified, of a subject-matter that may be negative, that may invite, as you suggest a masochistic state of mind. I would only add, in part; that even in such a case the post-depressive co-ordination altogether necessary, we are agreed, to the creating of art, will have been affirmed, transmitted, however indirectly. To put it another way; when a discernment of inner states, however horrific, however dispensable by means of a sadistic projection, is stabilized in terms of aesthetic oppositions and balances and other aspects of form, some co-ordination, some bringing together, will have occurred at the expense of denial; and this bringing together will have required, at the fount, the shadow of a reconstructed whole object and part-object whose presence can at least be glimpsed in the very existence of an aesthetic result. Thus, a painting that represents violence, disintegration, provided it be a good painting, of the full calibre of art, should remain not at all unpleasant to live with, day in day out. Earlier on, you have distinguished between "the creativity, the projection of it" and "the exhibiting of the artistic product." I am not so willing to separate as entirely as you do for some instances, all the motivations in these two activities.

To avoid misunderstanding, I think we should remark that the fact that many people are disgusted or outraged by a new departure in art, does not necessarily have a predominant bearing on the intentions, conscious or otherwise, of the artist. In my paper I discussed the dislike of art from the point of view of the fear aroused by so vivid a comment upon psychical reality. Maybe, though, this is important in putting the artist on his mettle.

As to sexual intercourse as a process identical in its method with relationship to the art-object, while endorsing the interchanges between viewer and picture that you suggest, I would like to add that the relationship exists, as does the parallel, only because of the essential otherness, the character of self-subsistent entity, the complement to the breast relationship, that has been created.

Meltzer: We are agreed that the successful work of art is compelling; it induces a process in us, an experience whereby the viewer's integration is called upon in the depressive position to restrain his attacking impulses, for the sake of a good introjection; it means allowing the good object to make a good kind of projection into one's inner world.

[. . .]

I have said earlier that it is necessary for a theoretical approach to recognize the possibility of evil motivation in the exhibiting of art, that is, either as a means of projecting the persecutory or depressive anxieties connected with destroyed objects into viewers or, worse, as a means of corrupting and attacking their internal relationships. But I have also stressed that the motivation for exhibiting good works of art is derived from two sources: first of all from the desire to be understood and appreciated by others, as an important element for reinforcing the capacity to carry on with painful struggle toward the depressive position; and second, I have implied that there comes a point of stabilization in the inner world when that element of the depressive position that has to do with feelings of concern for "all the mother's babies" becomes very dominant. At this point, I believe, the impulse to exhibit works of art, representing the artist's progress in working through his depressive conflicts, begins to take a form that could rightly be called the impulse to *sermonize*. In this sense every work of art, from such a period of an artist's life, has the function of a *sermon to siblings*, a sermon which is not only intended to show what has been accomplished by this brother but is also intended to project into the siblings both the restored object as well as to project those capacities for the bearing of depressive pains which have been achieved by the artist in his own development. Seen from the spectator's angle, the viewing, and the yearning to view, the work of masters would not only derive from the relationship to the product of art as representing the mother's body and the contents of her body; it also represents the relationship to the artist as an older sibling from whom this kind of encouragement and help in achieving a sufficient devotion and reverence for the parent is sought.

Stokes: You have now carried further your contribution on the role of projective identification. It brings me a feeling of light, first in regard to a matter that has been of particular importance. Things made by man please and depress the aesthete through a mode far more intimate than in his contemplation of Nature. You explain it by introducing the projective identifications of which the viewer of art is the recipient. I wish there had been the occasion for you to re-introduce here from your Tyranny paper your conception of the smugness remaining in the projector of evil, and that you had brought it to bear in connection with a remark you made to me about the effect on us of much Victorian architecture.

As to sermonizing to siblings, I cannot refrain from mentioning that I found long ago that I could provide no other word than "brotherliness" to denote an interplay of equal, non-emphatic, forms in some of the greatest painting.

In applying psychoanalysis to the social value of art, to the manner of communication and to the role it plays in the calculations and satisfactions of the artist himself, you make a new beginning. It is from your angle, I think, that what appears to be the slavery of the artist will be most fruitfully approached, an aspect, I have pointed out elsewhere, entirely ignored by psychoanalysis. I mean the subjection of the artist to his time, and therefore to

the art of his time, inasmuch as art must reflect typical concatenations of experience, of endeavour, in the milieu in which the
artist and his public live; otherwise the artist's achievement of
form seems to be nearly always without urgency or power. This
cultural expression of significant dispositions both perennial and
topical (underlying the creation of significant form) that may
completely change the emotional bent, as well as the style, of art,
will have entailed a novel psychical emphasis. Since we aesthetes
are inclined to agree that the creator's prime social task is to help
his siblings with their conflicts in a contemporary setting, identi-
fying stress and the resolving of it with accentuations appropriate
to a particular environment, just as each individual on his own
is bound to do; since the artist's attainment of aesthetic value is
understood to be inseparable from what is both subservience and
leadership, we realize at once the penetration of your approach.

I fear that this may sound as if I thought a painter's work
must include sociological comment. Of course it is not so. He is
concerned with value in the inside and outside world, the value of
landscape, say, to himself and to his contemporaries, a value that
sometimes entails resuscitation of a discarded aesthetic tradition
as he looks with new eyes, conditioned by current ideas, not only
at Nature but at the art of the past. This application of the inner
world to outside situations accords with the sensuous condition
of art and especially with some degree of naturalism.

CHAPTER THREE

Modes of art and modes of being

Carving and modelling [i]

So we shall now attack the vital though confused aesthetic distinction between carving and modelling. There must be a profound aesthetic distinction between them. As everyone knows, carving is a cutting away, while modelling or moulding is a building up. Agostino's virtue will shed new light upon the high imaginative constructions which common fantasy has placed around each of these antithetical processes (imagination itself is a plastic agency, fashioning its products with fragments). Agostino's virtue will illumine afresh the field of visual art. For the distinction between carving and modelling proves to be most suggestive in relation to all visual art.

* * *

---

i From "Carving, modelling and Agostino", *Stones of Rimini*, 1934, pp. 108-109; *Critical Writings* I, pp. 229-230)

That distinction between carving and modelling[ii] is for me one of the most fruitful in the visual arts: it applies to all of those arts. I enlarged in this distinction in *Stones of Rimini*. I showed that in the early Renaissance there was an architecture and sculpture that is the epitome of carving conception. Also in *The Quattro Cento* I showed that there is constancy of life in early Renaissance stone ornaments, a tense communion with the plane from which they were cut. These ornaments do not give the effect of having been stuck there. On the contrary they are integral with their background plane. They appear to be more than decoration: for through them we witness powers in the wall on which they lie, just as his face shows the man. Whatever its plastic value, a figure carved in stone is fine carving when one feels that not the figure, but the stone through the medium of the figure, has come to life. Plastic conception, on the other hand, is uppermost when the material with which, or from which, a figure has been made appears no more than so much suitable stuff for this creation [...].

Work of this intensely spatial (carving) kind recalls a panorama contemplated in an equal light by which objects of different dimensions and textures, of different beauty and of different emotional appeal, whatever their distance, are seen with more or less the same distinctness, so that one senses the uniform dominion of an uninterrupted space. The intervals between objects have assumed a markedly irreversible aspect: there it all is, so completely set out in space that one cannot entertain a single afterthought. In visual art, the idea of forms however different, as answering to some cogent, common, continuous dominion that enforces the bonds between those forms in spite of their manifold contrasts, gives rise to the distinctive non-plastic aim: and this idea was inspired, above all, by the equality of light on stone.

* * *

---

ii   From *Colour and Form*, 1937 (rev. 1950), p. 31; *Critical Writings* II, p. 23.

My oldest contention in this field[iii] is that differences of approach between carving and modelling characterize pictorial conceptions as well as conceptions in all the other visual arts. (Stokes, 1932, 1935, 1937, 1949.) The carver, in a manner more nearly concrete, is jabbing into a figure's stomach. The compensatory emotion is his reverence for the stone he consults so long: he elicits meaning from a substance, precious for itself, whose subsequent forms made by the chisel were felt to be pre-existent and potential: similarly in painting there is the canvas, the rectangular surface and the whiteness to fructify, a preexistent minimum structure that not only will be gradually affirmed but vastly enriched by the coalescence with other meanings. What a contrast, this side of art, to the summary, omnipotent-seeming aspect of creativeness, to the daring, the great daring and plastic imposition that are even more characteristic and far more easily recognized and applauded, qualities that cause us to clutch at them, or that tend to envelop us. But it has also always been my contention that some exercise of both approaches must figure in visual art. Nevertheless, the greatest exponents since the Renaissance of the rare type of painting that reveres outside objects for themselves, almost to the exclusion of projecting on to them more than the corresponding self-sufficient inner objects, have had the least, or else the tardiest, recognition of their supremacy. Those immense heroes of painting, Piero della Francesca, Georges de la Tour, Vermeer (Gowing, 1952), were forgotten and rediscovered only in the last hundred years at a time when texture, the heightened expressive use of the matiere of painting, a substitute for pleasures in past ages available from buildings, was much on the increase. Their rediscovery, then, points to the connection between this care for material and a non-grasping approach in general, since it is not at all the surface or texture of paintings by these Old Masters that most characterizes, in their case, the "carving" attitudes to objects.

* * *

iii From *Painting and the Inner World*, 1963, pp. 15-16; *Critical Writings* III, pp. 217-218.

Polishing stone is also like slapping the newborn infant to make it breathe.[iv] For polishing gives the stone a major light and life. "To carve" is but a complication of "to polish", the elicitation of still larger life. Carving is a whittling away. The first instinct in relation to a carvable material is to thin it, and the first use of such material as tool or weapon required it to be sharp, to be graduated in thinness. The primary (from the imaginative point of view) method of carving is to rub with an abrasive. It is possible that the forms in stone sculpture which possess pre-eminently a carving, as opposed to a plastic, significance, have nearly always been obtained by rubbing, if only in the final process. However, it is not necessary for me to enter into a discussion of technique. I think one can hold that from the deep, imaginative angle, the point, chisel, drill and claw are not so much indispensable instruments of stone sculpture as auxiliary weapons that prepare the stone for the use, however perfunctory, of abrasives. The chisel and the rest facilitate stone sculpture: and, historically speaking, it may be that these instruments were adopted from wood carving and gem carving for this purpose, rather than invented for use on sculptural stone. But the only point I wish to make is that rubbing belongs integrally to the process of stone sculpture [...]. Stone demands to be thinned, that is to say, rubbed. Wood demands to be cut and even split. Wood is not only not so dense, but possesses less light seemingly its own. Typically wooden shapes are nearer to typically modelled shapes. Hence, wooden shapes need to be more emphatic. In contrast with the flattening or thinning proper to stone more definitely circular shapes are proper to wood, conditioned as well, in the majority of cases, by the rounding tree-growth formation of its grain. But the light on stone reveals the slightest undulation of its surface; and since no stone has a general circular structure, curves depend entirely on the care with which the block has been diminished. Such forms, though they may suggest the utmost roundness, will tend in reality to be more flattened or compressed than in the case of carved wood. Indeed, as we have said, from this lack of exaggeration,

---

iv From "Carving, modelling and Agostino", *Stones of Rimini,* pp. 112-115; *Critical Writings* I, pp. 232-233.

from this flattening or thinning of the sphere, the slightest roundness obtains the maximum life and appeal. The light on stone is comparatively even: no shape need be stressed: where complete roundness is avoided, the more it may be suggested. So the shapes proper to stone are gradual, to which sharpness is given only by the thinned nature of the block as a whole.

Carving is an articulation of something that already exists in the block. The carved form should never, in any profound imaginative sense, be entirely freed from its matrix. In the case of reliefs, the matrix does actually remain: hence the heightened carving appeal of which this technique is capable. But the tendency to preserve some part of the matrix is evident in much figure carving, and in the case of some arts, has given rise to definite conventions: thus, the undivided knees of Egyptian granite kings and idols. My example is a literal one: for even though no part of the matrix is palpable, the conception of it may yet be imputed to some part of the form. This is the inspiration behind many of the great hard-stone Egyptian heads. In conception and execution they are pure carving; of which the proof is that nothing, no nothing, is more meaningless, more repulsive, than a plaster cast of one of these heads.

Michelangelo's sonnet [v]

The best of artists hath no thought to show
Which the rough stone in its superfluous shell
Doth not include: to break the marble spell
Is all the hand that serves the brain can do.

The stone is opened by the sculptor, robbed, restored, transformed. Sometimes in the late drawings we may feel that excoriation stops in favour of a Quattro Cento caressing; that the pluckings-out of spiral and oval, womb-like, forms from the rectangular framework, cease. The form is good

---

v   From *Michelangelo*, 1955, pp. 76-78; *Critical Writings* III, pp. 44-45. Stokes cites A. Symonds' translation of lines from the sonnet in "Form in art" (Stokes, 1973, p. 111).

and un-robbed [. . .]. What rounded words this Virgin has from the angel at her ear. The square shoulders, the bent arm on the table-top, the rectangular pattern of a soft, voluminous shape, seem effortless, glowing. There is often the same poignancy where Michelangelo has emphasized – as sometimes from the earliest days – the roundness of the head: though massive, it remains the more tender of his plastic inclinations. The well-woven words, as we feel them to be, at the ear of the Madonna suggest for the design a quality of contentment even, a mood in which Michelangelo may sometimes have come away from conversing with Vittoria Colonna. He depended on her high-born piety: doubtless in company with that dependence there existed the wavering belief that he, Michelangelo, put goodness into her: and it is likely that a rare conversational encounter of this kind was the nearest approach he could make to marital enjoyment.

The famous lines in Michelangelo's sonnet reveal the conviction that the sculptor projects no absolute form: his skill and imagination are needed to uncover something of the myriad forms the stone contains. He removes the twigs which conceal a bird on a nest. [...] As well as fantasies of propinquity we may expect in the context of carving, fantasies parallel to those of exploring the inside of the mother's body, perhaps of snatching a future rival from her womb or of appropriating a fruitfulness that the aggressive infant cannot otherwise attribute to himself. The attack goes on in sculpture, blatantly, one might say, since it will not be mastered unless fully accepted. The form in the stone must first be released or stolen, then exalted. It is as if while discovering the whole, much longed-for object, the infant were able to perpetuate this vision by those very same aggressive fantasies, perhaps of robbing the fruitful womb, which have contributed to his sense of loss and to his need of making restitution. Art is what it is from the character of being an act of reparation that may employ the entire contradictory man. The sculptor controls a rich hoard, animates at the same time an obdurate dead material, a catastrophic avalanche – "He breaks the marble spell" according to Michelangelo's sonnet;

on the other hand, much of his sculpture seems to state that the outer stone is not to be considered as mere husk: it too has forms in embryo.

Even in early, more finished works, he chose to preserve some evidence of the original block: the tendency grew to leave surfaces uncut or roughly cut. The homogeneous block could be homogeneous in a manner he valued, whereas the particularity of any form prised out of it became, after a certain advanced point, less complete as it was "finished".

In circumstances that might have entailed paralysing uncertainty, Michelangelo pressed on to solutions (aided by chance) of which the world remains in awe. Of his genius, the enduring strength of his vision, we can only remark feebly, tautologically, that his grip on life was thus strong. He valued in sculpture parts of the rough stone that will collaborate in revealing the particular nude; uncover the emotional process of searching the block; add to depth and vivification; allow the worked forms to suggest both emergence and shelter, a slow uncoiling that borrows from the block the ideal oneness, timelessness, singleness of pristine states.

Pregnant shapes [vi]

We approach one aspect of Quattro Cento sculpture. For the Agostino reliefs in the Tempio [Malatestiano, at Rimini] have the appearance of marble limbs seen in water. From the jointure of so many surfaces as are carved in these reliefs, from the exaggerated perspective by which they are contrived, from the fact that though bas reliefs they suggest forms in the round, we are reminded of those strange elongations of roundness, those pregnant mountings up and failings away of flatness, those transient foreshortenings that we may see in stones sunk in clear waters, in the marble floors themselves of baths; we

---

vi From "The Mediterranean", *Stones of Rimini*, pp. 97-99; *Critical Writings* I, pp. 223-225.

experience again the potential and actual shapes of the stone in water, changing its form, glimmering like an apparition with each ripple or variation of light. But whereas we pick the stone out of the tide or tread the bath floor to discover its real shape, Agostino's forms never cease to be potential as well as actual. Yet this suggested potentiality causes no hiatus in the impression they afford. These shapes are definite enough, unequivocal: only they have as well the quality of apparition which, so far from mitigating the singleness of their impact on the eye, makes them the more insistent and even unforgettable. They glow, luminous in the rather dim light of the Tempio. Their vitality abounds. The life, the glow of marble has not elsewhere been dramatized thus. For, by this peculiar mode of bas relief in which forms in the round are boldly flattened out, the pregnant functions imputed to stone in its relation with water are celebrated with all the accumulated force of Mediterranean art. These reliefs are the apotheosis, not only of Sigismondo who built the Tempio, and of Isotta his mistress, but of marble and limestone and all the civilizations dependent upon their cult.

Pregnant shapes of such a kind are possible only in relief carving. We begin to understand how, at its first elaboration, perspective science was the inspiration, the true and deep inspiration, and not merely the means, of Renaissance art; why it was the early Renaissance carvers, rather than the painters, who discovered and elaborated this science. We begin to understand how it is that what I have called Quattro Cento sculpture, with its stone-blossom and incrustation, with its love of stone, of movement, liquid and torrential movement within the stone (needing perspective to measure distance), with its equal love to carve shells and growth and steady flower, should be considered the core and centre of the Renaissance. The Renaissance is a gigantic yet concentrated reassertion of Mediterranean values. The diverse cultures of all the centuries since classical times were commandeered for this expression, and thus reinforced the imitation of classical modes, themselves of several periods. Thousands of years of art were employed in this furore. But again, the core, the central fury, was the love of concrete objects. Each diverse Mediterranean feeling for stone found a new vehemence. And of those feelings of which I write throughout these volumes, I consider the most fundamental one to be connected with the interaction of stone and water. In a sense, the fecund stone-blossom is already connect with some association of moisture in the stone.

Identity in difference [vii]

I dentity in difference is often realized by the few masters of today through a kind of addition and subtraction that the eye performs upon the colours used in the picture. I shall return again to this propensity of the eye, for it is most important to my argument. The invitation to addition and subtraction of colour [. . .] is a very ancient practice in painting, but it is sometimes employed today in a manner unembarrassed by the demands of exact or even partial representation. I shall refer cursorily to a semi-representational Picasso recently exhibited at the Rosenberg galleries. The picture is called *Woman with a Mandoline*. On looking at this picture one will perceive immediately that there exists some integrating relation, more intense than the one usually described under the words "design" or "composition", between the figure and the chair on which she sits. This relationship depends upon a little addition sum that the eye unconsciously performs (and the eye delights in this exercise). If the area of colour of the figure's deep red dress is added to the area of pinkish colour of her flesh, the resultant colour would equal In tone the light-blue armchair on which she sits. Further, take this red and blue, their respective areas and shapes, and we shall find that the purple-brown part of her headdress gives some sort of equivalent, both in form and in colour. Or again the black and purple-brown

---

vii   From *Colour and Form*, 1950, p. 49; *Critical Writings* II, p. 34.

headdress is a concentration or addition of the background colours that are divided into three zones. The point is not that an analysis on these lines should be literally true of the painting, but that this mode of interchange, fructification, metamorphosis, in terms of hue or tone or intensity, or by two of them, or by all three, should be suggested; not that a colour scheme should be thought out by the artist on these lines but that a conception of form, in turn based upon the family character of colour, should lead him instinctively to create a design thus integrated. In terms of two forms "going into" a third, of one texture as the sum of another of larger area and so on, there is perhaps expressed the wished-for stabilizing, not so much of our personalities as of its qualification by those miscellaneous mixed-up archetypal figures within us, absorbed in childhood, that are by no means at peace among themselves.

The evening light [viii]

An uncompeting relationship between two shapes is one in which neither shape is subservient, in which each enhances the other to a more or less equal extent. Thus, from the angle of colour whence this conception of form is derived, although one colour "shows off " the rest, it should be itself thereby "shown off": between colours, activity and passivity should be equally divided; and similarly between forms. It follows that in such presentation we feel that even the mass or the form of a picture as a whole is not so much a unit standing over against us, inducing the bipolarity of tactile sensation, as a more independent self-orientated and productive mechanism equally active in all its parts, with a small wheel (one part), as it were, communicating power to a conglomeration of much larger machinery and thereby contriving for itself a place in the unity of insistence by which colour is best seen; but only because also, unlike the part of a machine, it receives power from those

viii From *Colour and Form*, 1950, pp. 52-54; *Critical Writings* II, pp. 35-36.

very brother parts to which it communicates power. A better analogy, therefore, is the one of the human body. Thus, there is a movement between colours, a simple progression in the case of adjacent hues, one more complicated in the case of an area, for instance, into which other areas "add up" or from which they emerge possessing further relationships between themselves. But the movement has nothing except its own organic momentum, and, unlike plastic rhythm, it is not, at each change of tempo or direction, dependent as well upon a new polar relation to our own bodies.

As a rule, of course, a compromise exists between the carving and modelling mode, even in bad pictures. But often it is evident that a painter has done all he can with dazzling changes of tone to prevent us grasping all the forms at once. This he does in the interests of stress and strain and harsh rhythms (or even of mass) that show their strength by mounting and passing the peaks of opposition on which the eye bumps. He thinks he is interested in the purest spatial form. To my mind he is interested in form and movement that is temporal and incompletely transmuted to visual terms. But I have already admitted the value of plastic approach in the material it brings to carving approach. My bias is certainly in favour of the latter, whose products seem to me the crown of visual art. I would not deprecate the plastic approach, were the other a quarter as well understood.

[. . .]

The accumulated material of plasticity must finally be used to realize carving conception. A line is something we reach out to, a raft for the floating spirit. But colour properly used contributes to shape an outwardness or otherness. It is a more complete, more inclusive, and indeed more courageous, sublimation.

We all arrive at this discovery towards the end of the day when in the evening the things around, at which we have glanced, finally arrest us by standing minutely described. Things now have their own light: they seem less lit from the sky. They do not stand out in a sea of shapes: all shapes stand together, separate and in communion. The character of each texture appears encouraged by the equality of revelation at an evening sky allows. The eye comprehends, does not follow. Each thing is rooted: gradation is infinite.

Oneness and otherness [ix]

The basic architecture of the visual arts depends upon the many alternations such as repose and movement, density and space, light and dark, that underlie composition, none of which can be divorced initially from the sense of interacting textures.

Aesthetic appreciation has an identical root: it is best nurtured by architecture, the inescapable mother of the arts. Indeed, the ideal way to experience painting in Italy is first to examine olive terraces and their farms, then fine streets of the plain houses, before entering a gallery. As far as the streets are concerned a similar procedure can be recommended for Holland in preparation for Rembrandt and Vermeer. It is not a coincidence that what we now call Old Amsterdam was rising above smooth water in Rembrandt's day. Much existed on his canvas, in the character of the surface, before he started to particularize, to paint.

Now, if we are to allot pre-eminence in aesthetic form to an underlying image of the body, we must distinguish two aspects of that image, or, rather, two images which are joined in a work of art. There is the aspect which leads us to experience from art a feeling of oneness with the world, perhaps not dissimilar from the experience of mystics, of infants at the breast and of everyone at the deeper points of sleep. We experience it to some extent also from passion, manic states, intoxication, and perhaps during a rare moment in which we have truly accepted death; above all, from states of physical exaltation and catharsis whose rhythm has once again transcribed the world for our possession and for its possessiveness of us; but only in contemplating works of art, as well as nature, will all our faculties have full play, will

---

ix From *Michelangelo*, 1955, pp. 65-67; *Critical Writings* III, pp. 37-38.

we discover this kind of contemplation in company with the counterpart that eases the manic trend. I refer to the measured impact of sense-data that distinguishes the communicating of aesthetic experience from the messages of ecstatic or dreamy states: I refer to the otherness apprehended in the full perceptions by which art is made known. An element of self-sufficiency will inform our impression of the whole work of art as well as of turned phrases and fine passages. The poem, the sum-total, has the articulation of a physical object, whereas the incantatory element of poetry ranges beyond, ready to interpenetrate, to hypnotize. Or perhaps precise and vivid images, an enclosed world fed by metre, serve a sentiment that is indefinable, permeating, unspoken. Space is a homogeneous medium into which we are drawn and freely plunged by many representations of visual art; at the same time it is the mode of order and distinctiveness for separated objects. Musical ensembles create perspectives for the ear: as well as the "music", the enchantment, the magic, there is the exactness of rhythm, harmony, counterpoint, texture, and the enclosed pattern of symphonic shape, handy as a coin. We are presented with discipline, articulation, separateness, and with a blurring incantation that sucks us in, at the same time, gives us suck, communicates, however staid the style, a rhythmic flow. The strength of these effects will differ widely, but the work of art must contain some argument for all of them.

There is, then, in art a firm alliance between generality and the obdurate otherness of objects, as if an alliance, in regard to the body, between the positive rhythmic experiences of the infant at the breast and the subsequent appreciation of the whole mother's separate existence (also internalized), complete to herself, uninjured by his aggressive or appropriating fantasies that had caused her disappearance (though it was for one moment) to be mourned as the occasion of irreparable loss: there is the suggestion of oneness, and the insistence on the reality of otherness if only by the self-inclusive object-character of the artefact itself.

And so, these good and reassuring experiences, the basis of object-relationship, are used aesthetically as the cover for all manner of experience (i.e. they inspire conceptions of style even those predominantly hieratic or anti-corporeal and abstract, govern the treatment of subject-matter). This is the practical idealism of all art which says "in order to live we must somehow thrive". The artist is compelled to overcome depressive fantasies by making amend (often, as in the Renaissance, by presenting with an air of ease the surprising and the difficult), the amend that articulates together an all-embracing physical entity with bodily separateness, reconstructions of internalized good objects, threatened by the bad. Content, subject-matter, may be unredeemed; formal magic must rule over the pressures of culture. Obviously, art is not planned on tactics of avoidance. The artist has recognized our common sense of loss in a deep layer of his mind. Michelangelo, it is manifest, forged beauty out of conflict (not by denying conflict). The disguises of art reveal the artist; they do not betray him. It can less often be said of the activities of others.

These abstractions may not be so unfamiliar. The above conception of the Form in art has kinship under the modern dress with some well-known aspects of Renaissance theory, the emphasis on the human figure, on the proportions of the nude as the basis of all proportion including those of architecture; the welding of observation, of respect for the particularity of objects, set in space, with a mathematical or Neoplatonic homogeneity.

Classic synthesis [x]

I have thought it appropriate to refer to the final "happy" phase at this point because it helps us to visualize one of the many alternatives of his temperament from which Michelangelo's art proceeded. A passive inclination to which he finally almost surrendered, albeit with a masculine

---

x From *Michelangelo*, 1955, pp. 85-87; *Critical Writings* III, pp. 50-52.

austerity, contributed throughout his working life to the tension of his forms. A virile force was in control; for long stretches of his art, passive signifies encumberment and active, disencumberment. There is little sign, one might have said, before Michelangelo left for Rome in 1505 to work for Pope Julius, before the Laocoon came to light in January 1506, of that encumberment of his forms so evident in the Julian *Slaves* whose conception doubtless influenced the Sistine ceiling. Yet his journeying between encumberment and disencumberment was incessant: it will surely be agreed that no figure in the whole range of art affords so vivid an image of disencumberment as the marble David, disencumbered of clothes, of weapons other than the sling, disencumbered of the years. This nakedness, of course, belongs to the subject-matter and therefore to a thousand Davids, but Michelangelo adopted the poetic Renaissance conception with an unrivalled wholeheartedness: his still David of the turning head embodies disencumberment as never before nor since, not as a negative but as a positive state of earthy presence: disencumbered of cheers, of fame, even of the conquest which he has yet to perform. In this idealized presentation of a palpable, nerve-filled body, we encounter the classic synthesis between ancient experiences of what is undifferentiated or absolute and ancient experiences of what is particularized, a conjunction that is part and parcel of the formal elements in every art. No wonder that in Florentine eyes so attuned a David became the image of political, everyday Freedom. Athenian statuary with a similar self-possessiveness had once provided the same thought.

We are bound, then, to attribute to the weight of Michelangelo's figures of early date – to the Cascina drawings, for instance – and to the huge energy that liberates them, the character of encumberment disenthroned: inheriting themes of naked energy, of brute strength from Pollaiuolo and Signorelli, Michelangelo transformed oppressive weight into the breadth and pumping power of the thorax especially, into muscles that renew themselves by partaking of bulk. The machine for crushing becomes the instrument for lifting, for release. Guilt, bad internal objects, are identified with the oppression of marble weight, redemption with an easing, but in a sense ever so stupendously muscular, that there are no overtones either of smugness or of romantic enthusiasm for striving *per se*. Faces are not contorted with suffering or effort; indeed, faces are of much less significance than torsos to the artist: many drawings, apart from the studies of movement, show this to be so, none more clearly than the careful design for the first carving of the Minerva Christ. Thus, in the drawings especially, the human frame, rather than the features, represents the person; and often, it seems to us, the state of predicament in which Michelangelo passed his life, transubstantiated by this genius of great fortitude into an ideal condition of slow, perhaps cumbersome, disembarrassment.

I have particularly in mind the four unfinished *Giants* (*Slaves*) who wrestle with their stones, with time, with eternity, in the Accademia at Florence. I am suggesting that in support of Michelangelo's sense of predicament and guilt there existed a state of uneasy passivity, known to us in terms of an oppressive weight which, however frightening, had at one time been partly welcome. One of the so-called *Slaves* or *Captives* of the Louvre, perhaps the most typical of Michelangelo's surviving major works, is bound, tied. (According to the first plan of 1505 for the Julian tomb, it seems that there were to have been sixteen of these prisoners as they are named by Condivi and Vasari.) They are figures of passivity or suffering, and also of unusual strength. We are not made to feel that strength evaporates; though death will overcome it, the strength still shows, or, rather, the vision remains, as if coming from profound sleep. Indeed, while phantoms possess the *Captives*, a nightmare of pound-by-pound oppressiveness, their raised, bull-strong bodies translate some of this dependence into the slow particles of health The so-called *Dying Captive* of the Louvre is a relaxed image. He submits tenseless to his dream, yet sustains with the huge, refulgent orbit of his form the vigilance of light. His beauty is the one of a sea-cave's aperture that allows and withstands reverberating waves within . . .These beautiful forms, foreign to self-pity or to sentiment, are the product of deprivation, surrender, revolt, enlisted by an idealizing yet naturalistic art.

The line of equivalence [xi]

Classicism in the sense of a truly Mediterranean art, while keeping the broad grasp and the dignity associated with the wider use of the word, is "close to nature", far closer than is a great deal of romantic art which treats of nature as a raw projection of emotional states, of the inside man. This classical art springs from a precise love and a passionate identification with what is other, insisting upon an order there, strong, enduring and final as being an other thing, untainted by the overt gesture, without the summary treatment, without the arrière pensée of "thinking makes it so".

[. . .]

I have used the art of Cézanne to descant upon a continuous relation between emotion and the outer world. A stress on any point or points of the line of this equivalence (divided roughly, very roughly and artificially, into the two zones classical and romantic) determines both the quality of an artist's emotion and the kind of object he selects. The terms, especially outside historical Europe, have little meaning apart from a context. They are without precision and express as an antithesis what is in fact a gradual differentiation. They are, however, indispensable because by their means we can sometimes characterize broadly the artist and his object. Though our concern is wider than specific art, they were introduced in order to illumine the equivalence where it is best acknowledged.

Like the difference between these two terms, so the difference between art and life is one only of degree, if living is conceived as the multiform of expression. Artistic expression or communication is selfsufficient in comparison with

---

xi From *Inside Out*, 1947, pp. 109,116; *Critical Writings* II, pp. 174, 180.

the interlinking activities of life, of which art is the useless epitome. We need but to refer to another truism – a work of art is a communication in terms of the data of the senses – to point to a certain rivalry here with the exposed otherness of the external world. Not only is a work of art, as a datum of a sense or senses, an object in the literal meaning, but that object expresses the universal desire to translate life into an outward attachment.

The invitation in art [xii]

Structure is ever a concern of art and must necessarily be seen as symbolic, symbolic of emotional patterns, of the psyche's organization with which we are totally involved. This reference of the outer to the inner has been much sharpened by psychoanalysis, which tells, for instance, of parts of the self that are with difficulty allied, that tend to be split off, and of internal figures or objects that the self has incorporated, with which it is in constant communication or forcible excommunication. Pattern and the making of wholes are of immense psychical significance in a precise way, even apart from the drive towards repairing what we have damaged or destroyed outside ourselves.

In distinction from projections that ensue upon any perceiving, aesthetic projection, then, contains a heightened concern with structure. The contemplation of many works of art has taught us this habit. I think it is so strong only because in every instance of art we receive a persuasive invitation, of which I shall write in a moment, to participate more closely. In this situation we experience fully a correlation between the inner and the outer world which is manifestly structured (the artist insists). And so, the learned response to that invitation is the aesthetic way of looking at an object. Whereas for this context it is simpler to speak of structure, of formal relations, such a presentation is far

---

xii From *The Invitation in Art*, 1965, pp. 13-26; *Critical Writings* III, pp. 268-276.

too narrow. Communication by means of precise images obtains similarly in art a wider reference whenever the artist has created for the experience he describes an imagery to transcend it, to embrace parallel kinds of experience that can be sensed. Poetic analogy or image is apt; felicitous overtones coexist; the musical aptness of expression hazards wider conjunctions than those immediately in mind.

In visual art, too, we see without difficulty that form and representation enlarge each other's range of reference. Similarly, the same formal elements are used to construct more than one system of relationship within a painting itself, and with us who look at it. Whatever the total meaning, the perennial aspect reveals a heightened close connection between sensation significance, that is to say, impact on the perceiving instrument as it organizes the data, and more purely mental content that we then apprehend in the outside terms of sensation significance.

[. . .]

I hope it is not an outrageous conjecture concerning perception to say that stereotypes for psychical tension may be projected thereby, and that these projections in some part may have reinforced the perceptual bents to which I am referring. In any case, whether or not immured biologically in perception, internal situations remark themselves therein. We are dynamically implicated with visual stress, particularly with the enveloping use that art makes of it. When the final balancing, the whole that is made up of interacting parts, is suspended for a time by the irregularities of stresses, these same stresses appear to gain an overwhelming, blurring, and unitary action inasmuch as the parts of a composition are thereby overrun, and inasmuch as the spectator's close participation, as if with part-objects, removes distance between him and this seeming process. Much of the attraction of the sketch lies in this situation, which arises also whenever we think we find the artist at work, in his calligraphy or flourish, his gesture or touch, and, even more generally, in the accentuations of style. I have particularly in mind the extreme example of Baroque paintings with a diagonal recession, invaded by a represented illumination, cast diagonally, that cuts across figures, that binds the composition as a movement of masses, without respect for integrity of parts of the scene, of distinct figures, voids and substances. A principle, a process at work, seems to override the parts. It is one aspect of the "painterly" concept formulated by Wölfflin, in which values of what some psychologists have called "the visual field" dominate certain values in "the visual world" of ordinary, everyday, perception. We very often associate creativeness first of all with an ability to disregard an order elsewhere obtained, to ignore an itch for finality in favour of a harder-won integration whose image may still suggest an overpowering process, no less than its integration with other elements.

Hence the invitation in art, the invitation to identify empathically, a vehemence beyond an identification with real-ized structure, that largely lies, we shall see more fully, in a work's suggestion of a process in train, of transcending stress, with which we may immerse ourselves, though it lies also in that capacious yet keen bent for aptness, for the embracing as a singleness of more than one content, of one mode for "reading" the elements of its construction, to which I have already referred in regard to form and image. Though they always have the strong qual-ity of co-ordinated objects on their own, the world's artifacts tend to bring right up to the eyes the suggestion of procedures that reduce the sense of their particularity and difference; even, in part, the difference between you and them, though the state with which a work is manifestly concerned be the coming of the rains, or redemption and damnation, or the long dominance of the dead. Most painting styles are what we call conceptual: objects are rendered under conformity to an idea of their genus, to hierarchic conceptions (with a comparative neglect of individ-ual attributes and changing appearances) favouring the power to lure us into an easy identification with an expression of attitude or mood. The depicting of incident thus receives a somewhat timeless imprint, offers a relationship that at first glance saps the symbolism of an existence completely separate from ourselves. As we merge with such an object, some of the sharpness that is present when differentiation of the inner from the outer world is

more accentuated, the sharpness and multiplicity of the introjec-
tory-projectory processes, are at first minimized. Yet I shall note,
on the other hand, that under the spell of this enveloping pull,
the object's otherness, and its representation of otherness, are the
more poignantly grasped. But I want also to stress the opposite
point by indicating in naturalistic styles, which boast far greater
representation of the particular and of the incidental, that these
works, if they are to be judged art, must retain, and indeed must
employ more industriously, procedures to qualify the intima-
tion of particularity, to counter the strong impression of events
entirely foreign to oneself by an impression of an envelopment
that embraces distinctiveness.

I now call the envelopment factor in art – this compelling
invitation to identify – the incantatory process. I have often written of it, principally in terms of part-object relationship, particularly of the prime enveloping relationship to the breast where the
work of art stands for the breast. I adopt the word "incantatory"
to suggest the empathic, identificatory, pull upon adepts, so that
they are enrolled by the formal procedures, at any rate, and then
absorbed to some extent into the subject-matter on show, a relationship through whose power each content in the work of art can
be deeply communicated. I shall try to indicate further methods
and characteristics of visual art whereby the incantatory process
comes into being. I believe that much formal structure has this
employment, beside entirely other employment, and that a part
of the total content to be communicated: is often centred upon
unitary or transcending relationships, though they contrast with
the work's co-ordination between its differing components, this,
another content no less primary, whereby the integration of the
ego's opposing facets and the restored, independent object can
be symbolized. I believe that the incantatory quality results from
the equation enlisted between the process of heightened perception by which the willing spectator "reads" a work of art – often
with a difficulty of which the artist makes use to rivet attention
to his patterns – and inner as well as physical processes; an equation constructed or reinforced by at least an aspect of the formal
treatment that encourages the sense of a process in action. There

is vitality in common that suggests an unitary relationship, as if the artifact were a part-object.

I shall continue to touch on a few manifest elements in the case of naturalistic art. For it goes without saying that dance, song, rhythm, alliteration, rhyme, lend themselves to, or create, an incantatory process, a unitary involvement, an elation if you will. Thus when I wrote of this matter in 1951, I did so in terms of the manic. During the next year, 1952, there appeared in the *International Journal of Psychoanalysis* Marion Milner's paper, renamed in the Melanie Klein Symposium of 1955, "The role of illusion in symbol formation", where, not only in matters of art, she emphasized a state of oneness as a necessary step in the apprehension of twoness. Her keyword here is "ecstasy" rather than "part-object". Her paper derived partly from ideas she had already put forward in her book, *On Not Being Able to Paint* (Milner, 1950).

Of the principal aesthetic effects an incantatory element is easiest grasped. By "grasp" I refer also to being joined, enveloped, with the aesthetic object. But whereas we easily experience the pull of pleasant, poetic, pictorial subject-matter – classical idylls, fêtes champêtres, and so on – there is not so much readiness to appreciate the perennial existence of a wider incantation that permeates pictorial formal language whatever the subject or type of picture. Similarly a poem, like a picture, properly appreciated, stands away from us as an object on its own, but the poetry that has gripped, the poetry of which it is composed, when read as an unfolding process, combines with corresponding processes in a reader who lends himself. Therefore my description is the incantatory process, since I feel that all art describes processes by which we find ourselves to some extent carried away, and that our identification with them will have been essential to the subsequent contemplation of the work of art as an image not only of an independent and completed object but of the ego's integration. Since, as a totality, it is an identification with the good breast, I have often submitted that the identification with processes that are thought of as in train allows a sense of nurture to be enjoyed from works of art, even while we view them predominantly in the light of their self sufficiency as restored, whole objects, a value that thereby we are better prepared to absorb.

The first power that the work of art has over us, then, arises from the successful invitation to enjoy relationship with delineated processes that enliven our own, to enjoy subsequently as a nourishment our own corresponding processes, chiefly, it appears to me, the relationships between the ego and its objects, though concurrently the unitary power, inseparable from part-object relationship, that transcends or denies division and differences. To take the instance once more of this last relationship from painting, light and space-extension can be employed to override each particularity in favour of a homogeneity with which we ourselves are enveloped. And so, such effects in the picture – their variety is vast – construct an enveloping *mise-en-scène* for those processes in ourselves that are evoked by the picture's other connotations.

It is easily agreed that pictorial composition induces images of inner process as we follow delineated rhythms, movements, directions with their counter-directions, contrasts or affinities of shape with their attendant voids, as well as the often precarious balancing of masses. Predominant accents do not achieve settlement without the help of other, and perhaps contrary, references; hence the immanent vitality, and a variety of possible approaches in analysing a composition; hence the ambiguity, in the sense of an oscillation of attention, that others have noted in the interweaving of poetic images. It may be thought that this will hardly apply to the representation of balance between static, physical forms as opposed to the representation, in which naturalistic art excels, of movement or of stress and strain. Such immobility, however, often involves a sense of dragging weight, of the curving or swelling of a contour with which we deeply concern ourselves, since we take enormous pleasure, where good drawing makes it profitable, in feeling our way, in crawling, as it were, over a represented volume articulated to this end; many modes of draughtsmanship, or of modelling, may invite a very primitive, and even blind, form of exploration. In one of their aspects, too, relationships of colour and of texture elicit from us the same sense of process, of development, of a form growing from another or entering and folding up into it. And, as I have said, we find ourselves traversing represented distances, perhaps enveloped by an overpowering diffusion of light. Finally architecture, possessor of many bodily references, mirrors a dynamic or evolving process as well as the fact of construction.

It is necessary to repeat that the unitary relationship between ourselves and on-going processes represented by the aesthetic object contrasts with the integration of its parts, for which we value it as a model of a whole and separate reconstituted object. In a combination that art offers, we find a record of predominant modes of relationship, to part-objects as well as to whole objects.

[. . .]

I have been describing the suggestion of an overpowering process in the painter's deployment of perceptual truth that has been largely ignored in the exercise of practical perception. I use the word "process" because the overpowering is felt to be going on by the spectator. I turn now to the major overall process, a reparation, in which both the good breast and the whole, independent mother must figure, a reparation dependent, it seems to me, upon initial attack. I believe that in the creation of art there exists a preliminary element of acting out of aggression, an acting out that then accompanies reparative transformation, by which inequalities, tension and distortions, for instance, are integrated are made to "work". I have long held the distinction between carving and modelling to be generic in an application to all the visual arts. These two activities have many differences from the psychological angle, first, I think, in the degree and quality of the attack upon the material. Similarly, this difference of attack is relevant to the old distinction between the decorative and the fine arts where an increase of attack calls forth an increase of creativeness. But if decoration titillates, ornaments, the medium, and if larger creativeness may to some considerable extent oppose its native state, I believe that every work of art must include both activities.

A painter, then, to be so, must be capable of perpetrating defacement; though it be defacement in order to add, create, transform, restore, the attack is defacement none the less. The loading of the surface of the canvas, or the forcing upon this flat, white surface of an overpowering suggestion of perspective, depth, the third dimension, sometimes seems to be an enterprise not entirely dissimilar to a twisting of someone's arm. I am inclined to think that, more than anything else, the defacement involved of the picture plane accounts for the tardy arrival in pictorial art of an entirely coherent linear perspective. From many angles, extreme illusionism is an extreme form of art, not least in the aggressive and omnipotent attitude to the materials employed. Many – every month many more – materials are now consciously respected, set-off, in our art today; thus made purposive, their naked character bears witness to an independence of these objects. We often deprecate an entire disguise of the canvas's flatness; we advocate "preservation of the picture plane". But whereas the paint, for instance, stays paint in such works, a large part of the impact upon us may proceed from the fact that the canvas is so heavily loaded and scored. Always the strong impact of which defacement, I am convinced, is an attribute. It is "seconds out of the ring" for every writer as he opposes his first unblemished sheet, innocent of his graffiti. It is even harder to begin to paint. With the first mark or two, the canvas has become the arena in which a retaliatory bull has not yet been weakened; no substantial assault, no victory, has begun. If a painter be so blatant, so hardy, as to fling, almost heedlessly, upon the canvas, a strong impact, he will at best create an enveloping or transcendental effect of omnipotence.

Pictures in a gallery, even the pictures in the National Gallery, make an ugly ensemble; as an ensemble the bare walls would be more pleasing. There is no doubt that the most beautiful ensembles of paintings are of those that are abstract and thinly worked, unaggressive in colour. A Ben Nicholson exhibition vivifies the walls on which it is hung. Some kinds of abstract painting, then, employ very subtle attack. But we soon reach the strange conclusion that if attack be reduced below a certain minimum, art, creativeness, ceases; equally, if sensibility over the fact of attack is entirely lulled, denied. The plainer tricks of perspective drawing can be easily learned and then imposed, should the knack be greedily appropriated without a thought for the numbing distortion of the surface thus worked, and so without aesthetic sensibility. A practised artist will have become habituated, of course, to his bold marks. But he cannot be a good artist unless at one time he reckoned painfully with the conflicting emotions that underlie his transformations of material, the aggression, the power, the control, as well as the belief in his own goodness and reparative aim. The exercise of power alone never makes art: indeed it reconstructs the insensitive, the manic, and often strangely, the academic. Art requires full-dress rehearsal of varied methods that unify conflicting trends. Such presentation causes composition, the binding of thematic material, to be widely evocative. This is more clearly shown in music than in the other arts. Musicologists tend to discover that, whereas construction is easily analysed from a variety of angles, the creative element, that distinguishes a coherent web from clever dovetailing, in general eludes analysis. Hence a vague appeal, sometimes, to "organic unity". I believe that it is possible to be more specific in speaking of the deep charging of these sense data with emotive significance, whereby the deployment of formal attributes becomes a vivid language, that is to say, symbols of objects, of relationships to objects and of processes enwrapping objects, inner as well as outer. The word "symbol" here does not indicate parallel structures, but structures wherein the component parts, though possessing no correspondence with the component parts of the original objects, are interlocked and interrelated with an intensity, sharpness, regret, or other feeling-tone that belong at least to one aspect of the original object-relationships, especially to the fact of their coexistence, interpolations, and variety.

Whereas the finished work, or the work as a whole, symbolizes integration, once again while we contemplate and follow out the element of attack and its recompense, we are in touch with a process that seems to be happening on our looking, a process to which we are joined as if to an alternation of part-objects.

CHAPTER FOUR

Mother art

Integrity of the outward object [i]

Architecture, it has often been said, is the Mother of the Arts. I hope to intensify the meaning of this phrase although architecture is usually subject to urgent practical requirements, and always to climate. Such considerations, and much else – for instance, the intellectual pleasures of coherence, the bodily references imputed to mass – are regarded here as the conditions, or in the latter cases, the modes, of an aesthetic aim which cannot itself, of course, be confined, as is so often done, to the terms of modes and media.

In front of a fine building it would no doubt seem irrelevant to think as follows: we were first one with our mothers; then, during early infancy we found repeatedly (and feared the loss of, mourned) our guardians as whole people whose composite separateness in large measure defined the unity of our own ... But classical architecture, we shall see, essays the reconstruction

---

i   From "The sense of rebirth (2)", *Smooth and Rough*, 1951, pp. 55-63; *Critical Writings* I, pp. 242-244.

of this outside character, this ego-defining object: thus there has often existed a rather self-conscious convention of providing inside doors with pediments, of decorating interiors with all the forms originating from protection against the weather.

In Italy I have been much alive to what I eat. I cannot judge how the enjoyment of food has stimulated architectural interest but I feel certain that pleasure in building broadens appetite, whether it be for the cylinders of maccheroni and spaghetti, the pilasters of tagliatelli, the lucent golden drums of gnocchi alla romana or for fruit and cheese like strong-lipped apertures upon the smooth wall of wine. We partake of an inexhaustible feeding mother (a fine building announces), though we have bitten, torn, dirtied and pinched her, though we thought to have lost her utterly, to have destroyed her utterly in fantasy and act. We are grateful to stone buildings for their stubborn material, hacked and hewed but put together carefully, restored in better shape than those pieces that the infant imagined he had chewed or scattered, for which he searched. Much crude rock stands rearranged; now in the form of apertures, of suffusion at the sides of apertures, the bites, the tears, the pinches are miraculously identified with the recipient passages of the body, with sense organs, with features; as well as with the good mother which we would eat more mercifully for preservation and safety within, and for our own.

A roof overhead is almost as necessary as was the mother herself. Ubiquitous for town and village, buildings seem vast in relation to ourselves: their lower forms are actual to the touch as well as to the eye. A house is a womb substitute in whose passages we move with freedom. Hardly less obviously the exterior comes to symbolize the post-natal world, the mother's divorced original aspects or parts smoothed into the momentous whole. We shall see that in line with the stress of classical builders upon exterior architecture, by their exalting with such abandon the strong ego-standpoint that may devolve from a constant admission of this whole other person wherein contrasting aspects are brought under one head, the ancients forwent the power to develop machines.

Art wins for connective activity a grain of the finality of death. The urgent outwardness, straining to substantiate an image of an independent whole, bears witness to the infantile, newly won, single object whose loss was so feared, whose being, however, imbues the forms of classical architecture. But this does not suggest that an identical basis should be attributed to the graphic arts, even in Europe where they have often evolved under evident architectural inspiration. Besides a repaired mother without, graphic art as a rule insists upon the spell of inner (often persecutory) figures that stalk the mind.

Fine building exemplifies the reparative function of art: wide feelings, we have noted earlier, that centre on landscape, on mother-earth, are particularized in houses. Primitive dwellings are caves carved by the elements. Whereas ploughing roughens and freshens the progenitor earth, raking smooths it for the seed that will produce our food. Also in architecture there are indispensable themes of smooth and rough. Both by agriculture and architecture, and very often in the graphic arts through the example of building, a sensitiveness to surface has been employed, the lover's or the infant's precognition, evoking from stone or from canvas a unity of forms which are felt to be pre-existent; giving rise to a carving attitude that contrasts with the projection of forms by means of the mere clay, itself of little moment, or if it is equated with the products of the body, non-pre-existent independently. I have written at length elsewhere of these contrasted yet always interwoven trends of the graphic arts. My greater interest has been for works conceived primarily from the carving side, since I value the meaning conveyed by the accentuated otherness, by the self-subsistence, as it were, of forms, rather than by those juxtapositions through which we are made vividly conscious of tensions of the mind. I have more concern with restoration, reparation, than with the versatile interior giants that seem to infect the artist's material with shadowy or stark power. If every work of visual art compounds the two trends, until our own day at any rate, there could be no doubt as to which of the two was the more evident, and the more at home, in architecture.

It is a common experience to observe through the expressive features of foliage a house as the structure of their person. Round tower, high roof and dome, the Hindu temple and the similar roofs of Chambord, the acrid, bellying chateaux of France where so often a maze of shapes, or else giant forms, a vaunted mass, are emphasized – such typical architectural sallies have their context, no less than the classical building, from contour and from climate. But in section, in detail, however forcible the effect of mass, whatever the stimulus of the plastic nerve, they resolve themselves, more especially for their inhabitants, into surfaces that are pierced by apertures with entry to a womb-like cave. The finer the architecture, the better this figure is re-erected, re-enacted, complaisant in climate and landscape. Soaring Gothic cathedrals may grossly spiritualize an image of the body: yet exuberance from stone in organic patterns projects these fantasies anew, fantasies of a kind that are inseparable, to some small degree, from any building with apertures or a change of surface. Pinnacles, shafts and phallic towers do not contradict the trend since, whatever their abruptness, they will be referring also to the incorporation once attributed to the mother. Architectural forms are a language confined to the joining of a few ideographs of immense ramification.

The landscape[ii] intimates union with the beloved. Colours, textures, smooth and rough planes, apertures, symbolize reciprocity, a thriving in a thorough partnership. The landscape's centre is fashioned by plain houses in a cobbled street, by the dichotomy of wall-face and opening. Dichotomy is the unavoidable means to architectural effect. It has, of course, many embodiments, a sense of growth and a sense of thrust, for instance, heaviness and lightness, sheerness and recession or projection, rectangularity and rotundity, lit surfaces and shadowed surfaces, a thematic contrast between two principal textures, that is to say, between smooth and rough. I take this last to symbolize all, because it best marks the "bite" of architectural pleasure upon the memory: the dichotomy that permeates our final impression. Such effects as volume and scale, each providing a separate sensation, are finally

---

ii Described in the previous chapter – an Italian village scene.

themselves the qualities of that smooth-rough disposal which we observe plainly in the simple Mediterranean house; best known, perhaps, in process of being built, before glass has tamed yawning apertures of velvet-smooth blackness which confer an ordered sense of voluminous depth, smoother than the plastered walls whose bottom courses are sometimes left bare, displaying the close packing of stones that were blasted from the rock upon the site. The roof tiles bring another quality of illuminated roughness: light and dark, differing planes, assert their difference in a marked equality beneath the sky, like an object of varied texture that is grasped and completely encompassed by the hand ... In employing smooth and rough as generic terms of architectural dichotomy, I am better able to preserve both the oral and the tactile notions that underlie the visual. There is a hunger of the eyes, and doubtless there has been some permeation of the visual sense, as of touch, by the once all-embracing oral impulse. Architecturally, we experience the beloved as the provident mother. The building which provokes by its beauty a positive response, resuscitates an early hunger or greed in the disposition of morsels that are smooth with morsels that are rough, or of wall-space with the apertures; an impression, I have said, composed as well from other architectural sensations. To repeat: it is as if those apertures had been torn in that body by our revengeful teeth so that we experience as a beautiful form, and indeed as indispensable shelter also, the outcome of sadistic attacks, fierce yet smoothed, healed into a source of health which we would take inside us and preserve there unharmed for the source of our goodness: as if also -- the apposition though contradictory should cause no surprise -- as if the smooth body of the wall-face, or the smooth vacancy within the apertures, were the shining breast, while the mouldings, the projections, the rustications, the tiles, were the head, the feeding nipple of that breast. Such is the return of the mourned mother in all her calm and beauty and magnificence. She was mourned owing to the strength of greed, owing to the wealth of attacks that have been made on her attributes whenever there has been frustration. Greed is excited once more but achieves a guiltless catharsis on this sublimated level. And so, we welcome the appearance or re-appearance of the whole object which by contradistinction has helped to unify the ego; the joining, under one head, of love and of apparent neglect which thereby may become less fantastic; the entire object, self-subsistent in opposing attributes.

Such victory (in the depressive position) needs constant renewal. During the earlier period, the infant is unable to bring together as successfully the loved and hated attributes, his moments of love and aggression, his incorporated figures of loved and hated attributes. Experience in art and beauty strengthens the ego, if only because balance, pattern, harmony, welcome a composite whole. Beauty acknowledges a binding theme (which art seeks out in any collocation), an identity compacted from elements, perhaps contrasting, that swell the wholeness of the whole. Beauty is a sense of wholeness. From the opposing elements that can fuse in the sublime, we may sense at peace the impulse of life and the impulse to death or inertia, so well symbolized by the inanimate nature of the material through which the artist conveys his fantasies and achieves on occasion for outward-thrusting Eros the perfection of arrest. By means of aesthetic pleasure we appropriate the material world without disturbing it.

Architecture draws upon the origin of all sense of wholeness; builds upon the deepest foundation. It is unnecessary for this context to discuss the aesthetic awareness of form, of proportion, space, mass, with their many practical references and physiological stimuli. I need only to remark that since the inevitable abstraction, the plain geometry of building, the simple volumes and lines, the prime shapes, are potentially so charged with feeling, this the public and unavoidable art of huts, houses, palaces, provides perennial examples for the abstract propensities in other arts; that architectural form lies at the centre of developed art though this be specifically and continuously apparent to us in the main Mediterranean culture only. Since the beloved was so calmly, so perfectly figured forth by the Greek architectural orders, much of our graphic art, paradoxical though it seems, took courage to serve naturalistic ideals.

This expressiveness and overt domination by architecture in European art must be related to a variety of European materials, particularly to limestones and to the Roman pozzolana; further, to temperate climate and the clear Mediterranean light. Even more than the Egyptians, the Greeks, especially the Athenians commanding the unrivalled Pentelic marble, insisted upon the smoothest of walls for their principal architectural style. Fine masonry of close joints was often plastered in order that it should thereby be the more smooth, the more radiant. An extreme care for simple surface, and so, for the smallest change of plane, and so, for apertures, was never lost, it seems, if we consider the continuity of Mediterranean houses. The monolithic look of their walls, doubtless borrowed, here as in other parts of the world, from mud construction, denies manyheaded chaos to the primeval cave. Similarly, every type of masonry and of brick may sharpen our sensitiveness to surface, to what is rough and to what is conceived to be less rough if only because it conveys an impression of vivid control.

Concreted time [iii]

Limestone, for the most part formed of organic deposits, is the link between the organic and inorganic worlds. Limestone exhibits in mummified state the life no longer found of the Silurian and other distant ages, just as the Istrian palaces of Venice present to us in terms of space, the hoard of ancient Venetian enterprise. The very substance of limestone suggests concreted Time, suggests that purely spatial or objective world which limestone architecture has organized for us. Though they have lacked the knowledge of limestone's origin, yet the unconscious fantasies of many races have directed artists to attain spatial completeness in their use of this stone. Except in terms of these fantasies connected with limestone we cannot explain either the ebullient life, the stone-blossom of Quattro

---

iii "The pleasures of limestone: a geological medley", *Stones of Rimini*, 1934, pp. 40-43; *Critical Writings* I, pp. 196-197.

Cento marble carving, or the complete and final revelation, the spectacular translation of time into space implicit in Quattro Cento limestone architecture.

The forms of life that are concreted into limestone, though apparent enough in many structures and in fossils, were never understood as such. Yet by some part of the mind their history was apprehended, and thus served to inspire humanistic art. A deeper love of stone than any that obtained in other periods, alone will explain those basic aspects of the Renaissance that are here termed Quattro Cento. And what is true of the Quattro Cento is true in some degree of Mediterranean art as a whole. I do not mean to suggest, however, that these obscure feelings would have made themselves felt so strongly except that some limestones not only have direct aesthetic appeal but also practical advantages for building and sculptural purposes. As is usual in what concerns the imagination, different fantasies, connected with the same object, go hand in hand, enhance one another's power. Any great love has many roots, many perceptions.

So let us consider the genesis of limestone. Lime, in the first place, is set free by the decomposition of igneous rocks which make up 95 per cent of the earth's crust. They contain on an average, it is reckoned, about five per cent of lime. This lime is carried in solution by rivers to the sea. Except under special circumstances it is not then deposited, since the amount of carbon dioxide in sea-water keeps the calcium carbonate in solution: it is, however, extracted from the water by animals and plants. The deposits of their remains are cemented into limestone. Limestone is petrified organism. We may see hundreds of shell fossils on the surfaces of some blocks. Nor are the animal fossils rare. The skeletons of coral are common, so too of the crinoid, a kind of starfish. These fossils were, and are, encountered continually in the quarries; and however falsely ancient philosophy and science may have explained them, art, which employs in a more direct way deep unconscious "knowledge", magnified the truth. Shells were a Quattro Cento symbol. They have a long history in classical architecture and sculpture. But it was the Quattro Cento carvers who in their exuberance contrived for them the import of momentous emblems. Marine decoration of every kind is abundant in Quattro Cento art: dolphins, sea-monsters, as well as the fruits of the earth and the children of men, encrust the stone or grow there. The metamorphosed structure of marble encouraged an extreme anthropomorphic interpretation of its original life. Needless to say, though marine symbols attained a heightened significance in the humanism expressed by Quattro Cento art, they are common to Roman and Greek art and to Mediterranean art as a whole. So we must contemplate the entire Mediterranean basin in order to interpret the Quattro Cento achievement. The sea and the limestone dominate those lands. The supply of fresh water springs from that stone. On our return from a visit to the south, we remember the lime-stone well-heads and the limestone fountains.

We begin readily to conceive the bond of classical build-ing and limestone. No other architectural forms remind one so much of the horizontal bedding of stones. The jutting cornice, the architrave mouldings, the plinths and blocks, have a definite relation to the joints of stones as seen in quarry or cliff; and particularly to limestone, medium between the organic and the inorganic worlds.

A Greek temple is an ideal quarry reconstructed on the hill.

Myth, stone, and water [iv]

Limestone is the very material of classical architecture. The Greek temple of limestone or marble is an organiza-tion, not only of the Greek rock, but of the soil and the spring ducts and all the fruit that ensues, all the care and labour they have demanded. This immediate kind of building, the distinct mass of column and column and roof, this ordination of shape and void light and shade, is the order, composed for classical man, of his space and of his light, and of his elements,

---

iv   From "The Mediterranean", *Stones of Rimini,* 1934, pp. 94-97; *Critical Writings* I, pp. 223-224.

all of which have their connection with the limestone. The temple is not white against the sky, but golden, a solid tawniness that suggests the strongest concretion of the process by which the grey olive leaf took nurture and dye from the limestone earth. Classical architecture is limestone architecture. The most fanciful, the most poetic and the most obvious connection of limestone with the elements is with water.

Homer speaks of "caverned Lacedaemon". Caves and grottoes, lost and disappearing springs, and the sudden meadows dependent upon their reappearance, perpetual rivulets upon mountain summits, fresh waters that appear from the depths of the sea, in fact every kind of water freak and water beauty ordaining the fantastic range and liquid poetry of classical myths, are characteristic of a limestone relief. In summer, fresh water was indeed precious. Water always needed care. The rapid run-off from the mountains saved the Greeks from the abysmal mythology of great rivers, of slow rivers and their regular savagery. In popular myth, the mountain streams that the sun destroyed so early, were the children of Niobe slain by the darts of Apollo. Fresh water was dramatic, a swift visitor, often subterranean in his entrances and exits, even submarine. Water was precious and clear, to be gathered, to be worshipped. So the limestone shrine mirrors the deep pool or forms the perennial fountain. What greater beauty than the stone instrument of space set about the clear pool, or dripping with the fountain, what more solid thing for water, for its clearness, its liquidity, than marble?

The ideas of marble and water are closely mingled in our minds. This connection not only reflects the influence of Venice, or of stone fountains galore, of grottoes and Baroque and Rococo garden play, of Roman aqueducts and wells and ancient baths: it is deeper, it reflects the whole vast field of Mediterranean building and Mediterranean influence in every country of the earth. And what beautiful things water does to stone, just as stone to water; what varieties are possible to their combination. I write of them throughout these volumes. Quattro Cento art is only one aspect of that preoccupation, the one I find most profound. In Baroque and Rococo, and, indeed, in most developments of the use of classical forms in southern climates, the alliance between stone and water is more definitely and dramatically, if more superficially, stated. Classical architecture, in the widest sense of the expression, is the stone architecture par excellence, for just this very reason: since stone that wants for an imaginative connection with water loses much of its significance. The water content, of course, was only gradually brought out and stressed and even isolated in such extravagance as the Baroque fountain and grotto. The link here is the use to which the Romans put travertine.

In the original classic forms, in Doric architecture, water content is immanent, unspoken: it helps the clearness of those forms to suit both Mediterranean sea and sky and land. The temple was not merely a structure but a limestone structure that people passed or entered. Behind it, historically, was the channel for flowing water and then the small rain-shrines that made their water still and clear and hard and potable.

Greek art and Greek life reveal the original classic attitude. Protestation comes later. There in the south, in space, architecture has always been the parent art; and consequently far beyond the south, architecture in any grand sense, and stone structure, have been synonymous. This begets a tangle for us in the north, one of the many tangles we inherit from the intrusion of Mediterranean values. For the use of stone in the south was by no means dictated merely by its superior permanence, as it tends to have been in the north.

Some writers claim to prove that the Doric was originally a wood architecture. But it is an entire mistake to view the Doric limestone temple as a wood structure copied in a more permanent and costly material. For the supply of wood is, and was, often limited in the Mediterranean basin. Most Greek states had difficulty in procuring suitable wood to build their ships. They traded for wood. Stone, on the other hand, limestone, was the stuff of many districts. Whatever the origin of the Doric, it soon became a limestone expression, in some sense proclaiming the prevalence of this stone; so that we cannot imagine any profanation by wood within or without the temple. Again, limestone is warm, takes the light: it is the immediate object, the touchable mass object symbolizing the passage of the southern day: and water closely sips the marble.

Refracted light through clear water throws marble into waves, tempers it with many dimensional depths. Hence the poignancy of submerged temples, or of an Aphrodite's marble arm dragged over the clear and elongating pebbles by the nets of Cnidian fishermen.

The flux of feelings objectified [v]

I write of stone. I write of Italy where stone is habitual. Every Venetian generation handles the Istrian stone of which Venice is made. Venetian sculpture proceeds now, not by chisel and hammer, but under the hands, the feet, under the very breath of each inhabitant and of a few cats, dogs and vermin. See the knobs upon the Ponte della Paglia, how fine their polish, how constantly renewed is their hand-finish.

Hand-finish is the most vivid testimony of sculpture. People touch things according to their shape. A single shape is made magnificent by perennial touching. For the hand explores, all unconsciously to reveal, to magnify an existent form. Perfect sculpture needs your hand to communicate some pulse and warmth, to reveal subtleties unnoticed by the eye, needs your hand to enhance them. Used, carved stone, exposed to the weather, re cords on its concrete shape in spatial, immediate, simultaneous form, not only the winding passages of days and nights, the opening and shutting skies of warmth and wet, but also the sensitiveness, the vitality even, that each successive touching has communicated. This is not peculiar to Venice nor to Italy. Almost everywhere man has recorded his feelings in stone. To the designed shape of some piece, almost everywhere

---

v   From "Stone and water", *Stones of Rimini,* 1934, pp. 15-20; *Critical Writings* I, pp.183-185.

usage has sometimes added an aesthetic meaning that corresponds to no conscious aesthetic aim. But it is in Italy and
other Mediterranean countries that we take real courage from
such evidence of solid or objectified feelings, quite apart from
the fact that these are the countries of marble, of well-heads
and fountains, of assignation or lounging beneath arcades and
porticoes, of huge stone palaces and massive cornices where
pigeons tramp their red feet. We are prepared to enjoy stone
in the south. For, as we come to the southern light of the
Mediterranean, we enter regions of coherence and of settled
forms. The piecemeal of our lives now offers some mass, the
many heads of discontent are less devious in their looks. When
we stand in the piazzas of southern towns, it is as if a band had
struck up; for when grouped at home about our native bandstand we have noticed the feeble public park to attain a certain
definiteness. Similarly we are prepared in the southern light to
admire the evidence of Italian living concreted and objectified
in stone.

But exhilaration gained from stone is a vastly different
encouragement from the one that music may afford. It is an
opposite encouragement. Or rather it is something more than
the bestowal of a tempo on things. For tempo, the life-process
itself, attains concreteness as stone. In Venice the world is
stone. There, in stone, to which each changing light is gloss, the
human process shines clear and quasi-permanent. There, the
lives of generations have made exteriors, acceptable between
sky and water, marbles inhabited by emotion, feelings turned
to marble.

Without a visit to Venice you may hardly envisage stone
as so capable to hold firm the flux of feelings. Stone sculpture
apart, stone is more often conceived in the north as simply
rock-like. And who will love the homogeneous marble sheets
in the halls of Lyons' Corner Houses? No hands will attempt to
evoke from them a gradual life. For nowhere upon them is the
human impress. Few hands have touched them, or an instrument held in the hand. They were sliced from their blocks by
impervious machines. They have been shifted and hauled like

so many girders. They are illumined in their hues beneath the light; yet they are adamant.

In writing now of Venice, I have not in mind Venetian sculpture nor marble palaces reflecting the waters between them. I refer to the less signal yet vast outlay there of the salt-white Istrian stone, every bit of it used; to bridge-banisters and fondamenta-posts made smooth and electric by swift or groping hands and by the sudden sprawls of children; to great lintels seared like eaten wood above storehouse doorways on the Giudecca; to the gleaming stanchion on the quay in front of the Salute, a stanchion whose squat cylindrical form is made all the more trenchant by the deep spiral groove carved by the repeated pull of ropes; to vaster stanchions on the Zattere, lying as long and white and muffled as polar bears . . . Stone enshrines all usage and all fantasies. They are given height, width, and breadth, solidity. Life in Venice is outward, enshrined in gleaming white Istrian. Each shrine is actuality beneath the exploring hand, is steadfast to the eye. Such perpetuation, such instantaneous and solid showing of a long-gathered momentum, gives the courage to create in art as in life. For living is externalization, throwing an inner ferment outward into definite act and thought. Visual art is the clearest mirror of this aim. The painter's fantasies become material, become canvas and paint. Stone the solid, yet the habitat of soft light like the glow of flesh, is the material, so I shall maintain, that inspires all the visual arts. Marble statues of the gods are the gods themselves. For they are objects as if alive which enjoy complete outwardness.

In Venice, even pain has its god-like compass. Masks of toothache, masks of suffering, snow-white, incorrigible, overhanging dark waters, these great stone heads line the base of the palazzo Pesaro on the side canal. The gondolier who enters from the Grand Canal will need to use the masks to correct his black boat. He thus polishes one or two heads, damps the swollen cheek of another, strikes a hollow roaring mouth. The cries from canal and from calli, new noises that are caught to the clammy, still livid recesses of the stone, released old and thin and ominous as echo, are as sustenance to these perennial faces . . .

That a stone face representing Vice or toothache should be an assistance in navigation, that misery should be exemplified as solid, attaining beauty in completeness, lends to all phenomena, even the least welcome, an almost positive zest. And see how these stones make permanent drama of the sky's shifting materials! Istrian marble blackens in the shade, is snow or saltwhite where exposed to the sun. Light and shade are thus recorded, abstracted, intensified, solidified. Matter is dramatized in stone, huge stonework palaces rebutting the waters.

No: it is the sea that thus stands petrified, sharp and continuous till up near the sky. For this Istrian stone seems compact of salt's bright yet shaggy crystals. Air eats into it, the brightness remains. Amid the sea Venice is built from the essence of the sea. Over the Adriatic, mounted upon churches and palaces, a thousand statues posture, distilled agleam from the whirls and liquid tresses of the Adriatic over which they are presiding. They stand white against the sky, one with a banner, another with a broken column in her hands.

Yet this whiteness as of salt is not dazzling. On the contrary, though here the sea is petrified, it still is ruffled or is cut into successive cylinders and pillars. Istrian stone has always been hammered. It is a convention of its use which probably arose in the construction of bridges and water stairs. For this hammering, which makes the smallest surface a microcosm of the larger growths in light and shade, prevents the stone from being slippery. So, we are reminded of the substances that batten on slippery rocks and roughen them, shells with crusted grooves, or hard sponges. When such thoughts are uppermost, Istrian stone itself, Venice herself; is an incrustation.

Or again at night, Istrian is lace. The Baroque fronts are like giant fretworks that stiffen the brighter stars. Lace, in fact, has always been an industry in Venice, though more particularly at Chioggia where they have woven it large and coarse.

Again if in fantasy the stones of Venice appear as the waves' petrification, then Venetian glass, compost of Venetian sand and water, expresses the taut curvature of the cold under-sea, the slow, oppressed yet brittle curves of dimly translucent water.

Accumulated sea-change [vi]

Venice itself, as we think of it today, was a creation of the Renaissance. And it was at the time of the Renaissance and after, that the liston, the thin oblong of the most white Istrian stone, was set as an inlay everywhere, marking even the plainest apertures throughout the city.

But the first quality, as above, of Venetian building is sheerness and height. Opposing water at their bases, the palaces lean back. At water level, mouldings are so heavy and protuberant that architectural projections around the apertures aloft, appear less as projections than as incrustations at the mouths of caves raised above the sea, incrustations not only from the sea but from the moving springs within. So heavy are Venetian buildings at ground or sea level that they appear sometimes to he upside down, especially since it is rare that they are crowned with the usual projecting cornice. The untapering lightness of the higher storeys, combined with the narrowness and sheerness of the whole, affords a minimum effect of weight. Weight is below: foundations are visible, all that is raised above the piles; but these projections, like the roots of trees, suggest a rising sap and strong grip captured for growth.

[...]

In Venice as a whole, tone so easily acquires these values ascribed to colour. Thus blackness, as well as whiteness, obtains a meaning over and above its tone value, more especially that value fundamental to profound colour relationship, identity-in-difference. The gondolier's seaworthy serpent, we have seen, is black between water and sky: but rather than as a silhouette whose character is to stand out, and the character of whose background is thus to be a contrasting background, the black gondola appears in organic connection with its light surroundings, an organic connection, suggestive of circulation, which belongs to colour rather than to tone. This solid blackness seems to have

---

vi   From *Venice: An Aspect of Art,* 1945, pp. 1-11; *Critical Writings* II, pp. 88-96.

been extracted from the dark places of water which therefore now appear lighter. Similarly, the gondolier's rhythmic stroke sums in an orderly succession the crowded flood upon which he works.

[…]

The richness, the salt, the hardness of the water has caked into gleaming and hammered stones, particularly on rough days when the Giudecca's sea-green canal is tipped with foam. The past in Venice seems to be the period taken for crystallization: the store of Venetian history is encased by an image of an accumulated sea-change. So deeply laid are the imaginative foundations of Venice, to such an extent has stone abrogated the meaning of soil in our minds, that decay, as we have seen, takes the form of metamorphosis, and even of renewal.

Venice is a potent symbol of the mother. As we ride the canals we move within her circulation. All we have said of Venetian architecture reflects the same symbolism. It is not surprising, therefore, to find that it worked, that is, the oligarchical Venetian government: worked with more public spirit than did any other large political organization of those centuries; and lasted longer. History gives few comparisons with the internal unity of Venice. Elsewhere political sagacity has not combated destiny with such success: no other statesmen have seen so far ahead: and by means of the supreme realism of correct prognostication. Imperial Venice perpetuated herself, artificially as it were, for some two hundred years after her expected death.

Such artificiality in astonishing unity with such realism is the measure of all Italian civilization, but more particularly in Venice where nature in exotic form conspires with good sense. Ceaselessly the waters must be carved for carrying things, ceaselessly the lagoons must be marked and dredged. The immense toil of water portage is vividly yet slowly contemplated. The ruling classes, however luxurious, could at no time isolate themselves from communal life. Their palaces could not be apart or carriages at the door. They took ship or walked with others in the midst of the sea. Here nature conspires also with beauty.

Even ostentation here, even flamboyant intricate adornment, are often no less effective, no less utilitarian than a racing motor-car. Thus, no other kind of craft but the gondola, and so, none less beautiful, could navigate as well the narrow canals.

[…]

Sometime before this general magnification in   stone, on another shoal of the lagoon, at Murano, sand and water began to petrify at the hands of the thrifty Venetians. Apart from glass utensils and ornaments, at Venice, probably for the first time in Europe, glass was used as window-panes. The very translucence of water was fixed to palaces affronting the sea.

The feel of our structure [vii]

Appreciation is a mode of recognition: we recognize but we cannot name, we cannot recall by an effort of will: the contents that reach us in the terms of aesthetic form have the "feel" of a dream that is otherwise forgotten. This "feel" too may be lost until it is recalled by an action in the street by some concatenation of movement or of substances: in just this way much modern art offers us the "feel" of our own structure, sometimes overriding the communication of particular feelings, painting usually presents as well a specific subject-matter equivalent to the manifest content of a dream, in terms of an image of the waking world. The painter has been happiest when surrounded by an actual architecture which provided an assumption (a living style) that made it unnecessary to reconstruct *ab initio* for every work the rudiments of the body and of the psyche. Titian was adorning, not creating, the stone Venice, and Rembrandt the new Amsterdam. Architecture in the west has been the prime embodiment not only of art but of culture. There are left, of course, many beautiful places, many ordinary houses that are satisfying, particularly in the south; but it is not our ruling culture that creates

---

vii From "The luxury and necessity of painting", *Three Essays on the Painting of Our Time,* 1961, pp. 6-8; *Critical Writings* III, pp. 149-50.

them. Marinetti considered all the beauty of Italy an obstacle to his harsh idealization of the machine by which alone he felt enveloped in the unlimited way he demanded.

We will agree that the work of art is a construction. Inasmuch as man both physically and psychologically is a structure carefully amassed, a coalescence and a pattern, a balance imposed upon opposite drives, building is likely to be not only the most common but the most general symbol of our living and breathing: the house, besides, is the home and the symbol of the Mother: it is our upright bodies built cell by cell: a ledge is the foot, the knee and the brow. While we project our own being on to all things, the works of man, particularly houses or any of the shelters he inhabits, reflect ourselves more directly than will inorganic material that has not been cultivated thus. Of course buildings and the engineering involved, roads, bridges, and the rest, are so common as to be a part of a ceaseless environment. The ordered stone or brick encloses and defines: whether we will it or not, the eye explores these surfaces as if compelled to consult an oracle, the oracle of spatial relationships and of the texture that they serve. Hurt, hindered, and inspired by wall and ledge, the graphic artist has bestowed upon flat surfaces an expressiveness of space, volume, and texture equivalent to the impact, at the very least, of phantasies, events, moods.

Architecture has provided the original terms of this language that can rarely be put into words, though words may sometimes be found for the simple employment of the "language" by building when taken in conjunction with the natural scene. For instance, in the fascination of gazing along a dark passage into the outside light that invades an entrance, in a subject not uncommon for seventeenth-century Dutch painters, we may become aware that we contemplate under an image of dark, calm enclosure and of seeping light, the traumatic struggles that accompany our entry and our exit, in birth and death. To look along the walls of a cave into the blinding entry would be to experience a more dramatic symbol except for the consideration that a thousand threads of conscious life bring now to the passage and to the house, to the constricted brick or stone, an appropriate association. Seeing that the projection of phantasy on to all the phenomena of Nature is ceaseless, I would not deny that the "language" of form must have a far wider origin; but I would claim that the example of building, not least in view of a context in the natural scene, has greatly served the precision of that "language"; nor is it irrelevant that the graphic arts have been expended in many cultures on the adornment of building; nor that in pictorial art there has often figured the architectural organization. In almost all periods and styles buildings have been represented in painting; this is due not only to their commonness or to relevance for many scenes; a study of the employment of the architectural background in Renaissance art and in the theatre shows without question that they are treated as the emblems both of ordered beauty and of a psychological tenor, in general as the presiding example of the conversion of phantasy into substance and for bestowing upon phantasy an autonomous and enduring body.

CHAPTER FIVE

Close looking

Piero's perspective: art and science [i]

Piero [della Francesca] achieved equation between true science and a majestic rapture from the earth. We sense geometry and number expressing the amplitude of love: we witness an untorn naturalism: a universal myth that is apart.

Love and the love of perspective were one, the perspective, for instance, of tilted circular shapes expressed with the slow piety of very exact drawing. Yes, piety, but more than piety, far more than the Gothic bent for the encrusted curve of a gold nimbus, inspired the correspondence that is broad and temperate between his volumes. We have from him the widest vistas and therein the equal simultaneous constancy of things; a stillness that is not archaic, a fullness without boast, a massive self-contentment in the very stream of adult life. But he delighted also to show the virtuosity, as it were, of his rooted shapes in his fondness of temporary structures or of any such apparatus to whose related forms he could, like the dying sun on an autumn

---

i From *Art and Science,* 1949; *Critical Writings* II, pp. 195-198.

day, unexpectedly attribute a durable and selfsufficient sense. Similarly his men, even on the battlefield, in virtue of volume, of affinities between volumes and their intervals, vibrant, earthly, engrossed, possess the flux and the chance. Piero's science serves both to distinguish exactly each particular and to embrace it. Agitation borrows the broad arc of calm. The geometry is at peace with a deep-rooted organic structure, product of chromatic sense. Francescan forms are brothers and sisters at ease within the ancestral hall of space.

There are, then, three starting points for the critique of Piero's painting. First, the potential coincidence of science and art in the early Renaissance, founded on the new victories of perspective. Secondly, his sense of colour as the basis of his sense of form. Although connections are many between these two approaches, only the first has a literature. To the detriment of art-criticism, form is rarely envisaged from the end of colour. The two roads prove to be but branches of the third, the quality of love by which Piero's bare geometry is seen by us as warm and rich as well as noble; a nakedness of love, numbers that in bareness may thereby be clothed with magnificence as may the study-object of anatomist and physiologist, shared also by poets and by every human being.

Piero's forms are familiars, we have said. No form accepts sacrifice to the emphasis of another. Distributed by perspective they converse through spatial simultaneity, through their affinities that search it out. The postures of these forms acknowledge the same sublime homeliness. Angels and princes make themselves known with the slow gestures of a calm peasantry. Noble science gives more than the framework, gives undying accent to the straight mysterious growing of the countryside. Perspective separates, colour and form bring together in family circle the crupper on a horse and the shoulder of a hill, the fluting of columns and the hanging folds of a dress. To our eyes a slow majesty as of white oxen upon the white ribbon of a road between the terre-verte hills, belongs to the valley of the upper Tiber where Borgo San Sepolcro lies, Piero's town.

If there is an emphasis it is upon the homogeneity of space ignored by the medieval mind, an emphasis previously unknown to painting. Though a fraternal relationship between objects appeared in archaic and decorative art, the timeless unity of their space which could have permitted a wider divergence of family traits and a less summary organization, was neither comprehended nor desired. All the same, in the interests of that simultaneity, Piero, as did Cézanne whose sense of colour was equally dominant in his sense of form, preserved the two-dimensional character of the picture-space – a certain archaic flatness, then, of forms – in conjunction with a great depth and a great volume.

Piero suffered no contrast between man, his circumstance and his heavy body. The Francescan elders are semitic for the most part, hirsute, watchful, but it is as if their low raucous fire, subject to the architectural involucre of outwardness, cohered like a squared clod; as if the abysmal contradictions of the spirit were transmuted into the density and demarcation of a heavy turve. A transmutation, we feel (though not to the effect of those symbols that are so easily won in decorative art), a transmutation into the simultaneity of space. Space, to a less degree the perennial subject of all painting, was Piero's rigid concept: whereas conceptual art substitutes a convention for mathematical space.

When we remember his paintings we first think, perhaps, of broad calm heads, of an oaken calm, of head-dresses and blameless trees; of entablature, of foliage, linked as if by hands: of tufted ground and feet in profile on a marble floor, of open surfaces that bloom from open surfaces, spheres that respond to cylinders, fibrous hair to non-deciduous trees. No other painter, except Giorgione and Cézanne, transposed as completely his love of life into the terms of space. Other, and usually predominant values of visual art, such as rhythm, contrast, stress, movement, arabesque, are common to all the arts however differing their sensation in each. The great poet Botticelli, for instance, to our exploring tactile sense exposes visions, sometimes restless. The transposition lacks the finality, or any rate the immediacy, of space. Compared with Piero, Botticelli is as sea to land. One might say of all, or nearly all, the pictures in the National Gallery: compared with the Pieros they are as sea to land.

We are bound to attribute to Piero a deep contentment. The loggias and halls are not embellishments of princely life, but enlargements of an Italianate street, innocent of genre. His architectural backgrounds possess great beauty; but it is less likely we shall recall Piero when looking at St Paul's, or even San Lorenzo, than at the sight of a black-timbered farm building in the sun, a sublime demonstration of architectural meaning (since he has caused us to see it thus in element), with open doors and windows revealing a greater and more simple darkness. Outside, the sun, inside a generous darkness beyond the edges of neutral-toned apertures. The thought occurs of the square muzzle of a cow.

As well as his sheds, Piero's magnificent buildings are stalls of the greatest contentment. Their shelter is dignified, complacent, like the gesture of the Virgin in the Monterchi fresco, pointing to her pregnant stomach. There is sufficiency and amplitude both within and without the womb. Hills lie with heads, foliage with thorny hair, massive mouths on calm rounded faces. There remains always a strong ligament between light and dark, between what is spread and bark-like folds, between the rounded and the pointed. Each interval constructs an expressive pattern. In the stillness, apprehended at one glance, there is fire. The men and women of bovine lips and bovine eyes are gripped to their outward showing like trees in broad leaf. Above them stand the self-confident trees, circular, pyramidal, of thick foliage, nut, acorn, chestnut-bearing.

We may attribute a conscious application of such oaken character to the spatial settlement. Indeed, the Arezzo frescoes depict the story of the True Cross, grown from a branch of the tree of Good and Evil planted with Adam in his grave to sprout from him as did his chestnut-haired children. Further on, we observe this stubborn wood in a bridge and in a grained cross against the sky. At the last episode, the return of the cross to Jerusalem, the wood is held between two tousled trees, the link, it has been suggested, between the Old and New Testaments, between the many words that thus unstealthily would fructify.

If clothes are sometimes bark, hair is breathing foliage. Man, measure of the universe, on ceremonial occasions manifests the world's geometry. Hence the towering volumes at Arezzo of the hats. But consideration of pure form, in the case of such lyrical genius as possessed both Piero and Cézanne, men of roots and strong sensuous feeling, leads to no short cut, no summary artifact. Their geometry exhibited the condensation of their far-reaching love.

As is so often the case, Piero's theoretical writings mislead in the matter, for he wrote only of values responsive to rule, to scientific rule. These values, however, were in divine conjunction with his sense of the warmth between parent and offspring, between polychrome pavement and shod feet that create the spaces thereon, between grooved entablature and the creases in a band that rounds the head, between arm and peeled tree-trunk, horse and cloud, a small rich pendant and the wide spreading of lake and low hills, between a circular dark-toned hat and a porphyry disk, between hat, hand and battlement. Connection is always architectural in the sense of a division of an order: the mailed apple of a closed vizor and the rounded face of a trumpeter with his length of thin tube extending from his lips; the ring of a skull-cap and the spring of an arch; the darkness of an aperture circled with stone and the dark centres of eyes flanked with their whites; the consummation expressed in an emperor's conical hat surrounded by heads of coiled, pleated hair against a background of arches and circular disks; the spiral grooves of ears and the straight grooves of a transparent covering that falls from the head; the winding river with light paths and white belts or curving outer hems extended fingers and the feathered points of an heraldic eagle; the horses' hooves of opposing armies like wide-bottomed chessmen on the board; the acanthi of a Corinthian capital and the features and fingers of the Virgin, the beads and structure of her vestments; the dark head of a cross-bearer against the sharp walnut-shaped centre of the grain and the ribbed clouds beyond; in a crowd, head growing from head, half a mouth against a neck or a white hem disappearing against the white of an eye; the mounting risen Christ and a dark knoll in the dawn light; the hill-protuberances beyond Battista Sforza's ivory face and the diaphanous hills beyond her husband's warted cheek . . . The catalogue is mechanical, since the connections are not single but profuse, ramifying in stillness. Piero's colour exploits the affinity to which we have referred in terms of shape and tone.

All art exhibits connection, a bringing together. In visual art alone, and then solely in visual art deeply founded upon this colour-cum-architectural sense of form, an aesthetic communication may be explicit and immediate to the point of rebutting after-thought. It is the *réaliser* of Cézanne. Such demonstration of intellect and feeling was the crown of the Quattro Cento compulsion to make manifest. Thereafter the same chromatic sense of form to some degree persisted in post-Renaissance art refurbished, if we consider painting only, by Vermeer, for instance, by Chardin, re-enacted by Cézanne. Yet there has not been, and still there is lacking, a generalized apprehension of this side of visual art, eminent not only in painting but also in drawing, in sculpture and more particularly, in architecture whose steadfast forms and textures (not colours) have so often endowed that sensibility with archetypes.

Piero reveals the family of things. His art does not suggest a leaning from the house of the mind. He shows, on the contrary, the mind becalmed, exemplified in the guise of the separateness of ordered outer things; he shows man's life as the outward state to which all activity aspires.

The family of things. It is as if the poetry of deep affinities were identical with those objects and with their formulae; as if death's calm separation lent nobility to the pressure of each heart-beat.

There can be no art without something, however minute, of this quality; because Art, mirror of each aim, conspires to win for expression the finality of death.

Giorgione: catastrophic change [ii]

Many bad pictures are equivocal in their subject. It is unlikely that their painters for the most part have seen or even heard of the *Tempesta*; yet they are among the mindless emulators of this unrivalled masterpiece. The feeling of suspense belonging to the *Tempesta* encourages aesthetic contemplation in him who sees it.

Dramatic though it be, the background does not set a stage. Indeed, the figures do little. They are well to the front of the landscape, encased in separate thought. It is the scenery which enacts the scene. But this is not a landscape with figures: the figures are insistent. Nevertheless, we haven't any idea who they are or why they are there. They do not belong to the landscape in the sense of shepherds, owners or husbandmen. They belong in the sense of human beings belonging to the world. That is not a personal, but an almost universal, impression. It follows that the *Tempesta* is one of the most extraordinary of man's creations. The relationship between figures and landscape is revelatory; though neither landscape nor figures are simplified into a concept. Giorgione's pictures, relaxed both in subject and in treatment, are the opposite to hieratic.

Above the landscape to which the figures have their backs there is lightning, day and night near to each other, before heavy blue clouds taut sunlight that illumines the sides of buildings as for some memorable occasion. The new Renaissance buildings of Venice stand with the old, with the signs of war and ancient feud. Immediately behind the figures there are fragments of two small columns on a brick plinth; the cylinder and the cube, the bare bones of the new Venice.

The two figures commune only in the profoundest sense despite the new-won naturalism of their delineation. A stream divides them. They do not look at each other. The man looks past the woman who looks out to the spectator, glancing slightly down. She sits higher than the man who is standing, confident,

---

ii From "Giorgione's *Tempesta*", *Venice: An Aspect of Art*, 1945, pp. 52-61; *Critical Writings* II, pp. 127-134.

romantic, at ease. Though their positions would be uncomfortable for any length of time (the woman's pose, indeed, is an almost impossible one), they suggest an enduring strength, a strength of youth and a bond between them that will endure, just as they are more complete, they are more abiding than the fragmentary building of the middle distance. The woman suckles the infant. The landscape in which they appear unruffled, even the impending thunderstorm, are in one sense subservient to this firm-on-the-ground human vitality. Verticals of the trees incline slightly to the right, verticals of the buildings slightly to the left. The landscape is no decor, but the figures are at home here: it belongs to their substance. There are many affinities and approximations expressed between them, an organization, a philosophy, a romanticism which have ensued primarily from an acute colour sense. And it is, in part, Giorgione's jewel-like colour that determines the organization in a manner too complicated for exposition at this point. Chromatic conception of this kind may be broadly apprehended apart from its colour, from a photograph.

One judges the vertical by imagining a line down the centre of the man's erect yet turned body, that in itself is extraordinary. It is the architecture that inclines to receive the dazzling white light and it is the trees that incline before the air which goes as yet softly to meet the thundercloud. Without central position in the picture, without looking beyond any tree, here is the master of his fate. On the other hand, it is significant that the title of the picture is *The Tempest*. Succeeding generations have not found a better title. Yet, although there are counter-balances, in one sense the calm of the figures outweighs the value of the impending storm. They are present, future and past, whereas the storm is momentary. They are these things without pride of place in the picture, without the guise of gods or symbols, of primitive forces, or even of sempiternal peasants. They are young and buoyant people, without strain, without straining, harmonious. They are the classical gods in even more human yet lyrical form. Giorgione had no axe to grind: but he was foremost of originators in art. He broke down all the systems of insulation.

There has never been an art less mannered, at the same time less formalized. Accent was superfluous. The *Tempesta* is dramatic in the want of tension, it is lyrical, supremely lyrical by this lack of tension, by what the Italians call *ozio* or ease. Tension of some sort has otherwise always existed in art; and art will need it again immediately. For all other times an art without some tightness in organization, or even some looseness as the tightening bond, has not been art at all. Since Giorgione's time, western art is often skirting an abyss.

Once at least, then, a lack of tension was affirmative. The thunderstorm brews in the background, yet throughout the picture there is an equal and total insistence. Action of the land-scape balances suspense of the figures, a balance to the effect of utter parity in their diversity, dependent as well, therefore, upon reversed links; for instance, suspense from the flash of lightning (we await the thunder and the storm) and action by one of the figures in the very recent past. The woman has obviously bathed in the stream and is not yet altogether dry. She suckles the infant, an action of primal importance, for the mother as for the onlooker, inducing a sense of calm and self-sufficiency.

A painting with a dominant "effect" is jazz to this symphony. Both figures and landscape afford superabundant images of their interpenetration, and indeed identification, without any sacri-fice of their contrasting "normal" character.

It is time to ask: what were the conditions of this unique art for this ease or *ozio* that art has rarely enjoyed before or since, never to the same degree?

The first consideration is of lyricism expressing interchange. Giorgione's man belongs to the landscape, not in the sense of one of Hardy's peasants: on the contrary, in the sense of being at home in the world. Confronted by the rigours of life, by the opiate of thousands of years of religion accumulated to make life bearable, how came it that in the Renaissance "being at home in the world" was not but a one-sided commotion, not an affirmation merely of youth or pleasure or defiance? An answer must be deferred. First, we must consider what is meant above by "interchange". No less than the soul of poetry and, indeed, of all art; since the poetic is the essence of art. Often more succinctly than a "direct" statement, encompassing a vast range of meaning which otherwise would be incommunicable, poetry expresses something largely in terms of something else, owing to the association of images, of sounds and rhythms. Poetic synthesis, characteristic of all art, is a multum in parvo, a trick invented under the intensity of the stimulus. Any metaphor is an interchange of meaning.

We have seen a principle of interchange inspiring Quattro Cento architecture; we have seen that Venice herself inspires a lively sense of poetry, metamorphosis, of interchange, of inner in terms of outer. Giorgione's art, in turn, synthesizes the images learned at Venice. Nature, building, man, the *Tempesta*, shows all three impartially. Nature is more especially expressed by the sky, at its largest in Venice. From the Venetian air itself rather than the foliage we discern the seasons.

Leonello Venturi has remarked that Giorgione ascribed to the *Tempesta* landscape a drama of the sky that is common in Venice. At sunset the sky in the west is sometimes clear while banked-up cloud of a threatening blue holds the east. Houses looking west are perfectly lit, utterly revealed from the side by the sinking sun. Night strides on from the east. Giorgione has added the lightning, the impending storm.

He has shown the utmost drama of the soul as laid-out things. But it is poetry, calm poetry, not melodrama. He dreamt of the soul revealed, without stiffness or contortion, in the slow and durable forms of space, of relations between forms as the long contact of familiar minds, changing with the ebb and flow of light yet constant in their local colour. The two figures are not in a trance: they are amiable and serene, yet like the other Giorgione figures, instruments of evocation. Their thoughts meet, their minds meet, not their eyes. There is a pause in living: there is an interchange between past, future and the present, between the figures, between themselves and each aspect of the landscape, between a deep-set wordless dream and an outward world. Giorgione chooses a moment of utmost revelation, in visual terms sunrise or sunset when things stand "as they really are" and when the hush of this revelation induces a contemplative mood. At such time relationship and affinity between objects become an essential part of their meaning: every clearly seen object appears to possess equal importance, equal insistence whatever the size, owing to the interlocking palpability of local colour.

Imbued with this poetry, Giorgione dispensed with the grave formula. Although the hour is evening, he creates a situation of thunderous light where there is also dramatic change of tone to dramatize in turn the equal gaze of the protagonists. Moreover, despite this broad tonal range, despite this very first solicitude in art for the evanescent exaggerations of appearance due to the direction of their light, local colour is still intense, so that the calm evening value of each thing, though it be an architectural fragment or a building that crumbles – indeed, because of the cycles such qualities suggest – possesses added poignancy beneath the natural instruments of evanescence. In purging the whole of dominating drama, intensity of local colour dissociates the picture from the stress of a moment of time although that moment is vividly represented there; from a "situation", and this without neglect of naturalistic appearance. Indeed, technically considered, Giorgione's revolution was a huge stride toward the representation of mere appearance in its broad and hitherto neglected features. Hence the divinity of the ease of his spiritual disclosure, hence, by the lack of any stylization, the full employment of a sense of affinities that has not been equalled.

Without resort of later painters to a uniform flourish from the brush, evenness co-exists with the broad changes of tone which Giorgione, and Leonardo, were the first to use. Unlike Leonardo or any other painter except Chardin before the French nineteenth-century school, after choosing a kind of light for his subjects favourable to local colour, Giorgione harnessed true tonal differences or chiaroscuro to the service of chromatic organization. Changes of light, as a quantitive range, less subtle but infinitely vaster than the range of colour, those general and diffused changes in light unknown to his predecessors,

Giorgione dedicated to the service of local colour. None of his followers were equal to this subtlety. Although the Venetian school as a whole, headed by Titian, may be said to have used his discoveries, it was neither to the end of a greater realism nor an equal poetry but to the articulation of masses. As for the definitely Giorgionesque periods of these and other painters, they emulated and sometimes caught the poetry with differing degrees of vulgarism: sometimes light and shade were exaggerated, sometimes ignored, and the treatment was Bellinian. At the end of the sixteenth century, Caravaggio quite consciously broke up the Titianesque stylization of Giorgione's tonal inventions which had finally become a mannerism. Proclaiming a return to Giorgione, Caravaggio produced a dramatic realism. Yet Giorgione had employed chiaroscuro for exactly an opposite effect, for the contemplative, the poetic, pause. That is why his use of chiaroscuro is so enriched by colour. He is the father of modern painting. Unlike Leonardo, more than one aspect of tonal painting springs from him. Not only did he help to make possible the huge achievement of Rembrandt but he enlarged the scope of equal insistence. Venice, as we know, excels in black and white. Colour comes between, uniting them, uniting the vastest differences. It is a description also of Giorgione's achievement, a child of Venice.

[…]

He who has learned to find man's image in the wide wastes of the lagoon will he completely at home among the pleasant foothills of the Alps. I don't know how much is due to the intensity of Giorgione's vision of this man-accustomed landscape, and how much on leaving Venice for the slopes after a long sojourn, one would in any case he of similar mind – something of the vision is common to many who come from Venice to Asolo, to Bassano, to Castel Franco. It is no surprise to see the grove and the blue distance, or a Palladian temple at the foot of a hill, to feel that delicate detachment, that pensive, lyrical detachment, allied to an embracing identification which characterizes Giorgione's dream, touched with a little sadness. His was a young yet gestureless nobility attentive to all the long insistent harmonies of Nature that mirror the young soul. The poetry is purely reflective: there is not a shadow of a judgement or of protestation. It is the ancient harmony, the harmony of classical times recreated by a Venetian in the flush of the Renaissance. The Giorgionesque man is calm yet debonair, in an elegiac relation with his staff. A pensive yet untroubled beauty belongs to the woman with her baby. The young man, variously called a gypsy (from the earliest times), a soldier, peasant, a hero of a Greek myth, is the best lord of creation the world ever had. With his direct untroubled gaze he is the best representative of Western man. If the word "mystery", so commonly used in discussing this picture or anything connected with Giorgione, is introduced, one must know at once the complete dissemblance from oriental mystery and from mysticism.

Giorgione's poetry has an unforced ease, an uncontorted beauty. He put the soul into Nature and he did it with a better balance than any of the romantics (in any of the arts) that followed later in their thousands. What Giorgione felt and attained is of perennial importance: today it is more specially important. Again the veils have slipped: we stand between the night and day. We too must redefine the inner and the outer ...

[...]

In writing of Venetian fifteenth-century architecture and throughout these volumes I have attempted to show that the part of early Renaissance art I have called Quattro Cento possesses as a compulsion the character of all art to make the spirit manifest in outer form. Except for Piero I have called no other painter to witness. It is appropriate if an account of this aesthetic spread over several volumes and a considerable time should conclude with Giorgione, since the *Tempesta*, some twenty years ago, was the original stimulation. The *Tempesta* epitomizes the so-called Quattro Cento process, this self-celebration of visual art. Spirit had been brought down from the skies to inhabit a plane which the medieval world considered brutish. Spirit was brought back into Nature of which man partook, the old frightening home revisited in maturity. Once it was spirit forces, but now the fantasy of man, informing Nature. By means of expression, his perennial activity, the mind of man vies with the world in outwardness: deeper things come forward. An expressive token of all expressiveness, the face of the stone is made to show through the stone; and in the evening light there is a moment when mind seems to become extension, stands revealed to the eyes.

Nature is the mirror of man for the mature artist as well as for the child. But, rather than a symbol conceived from an object, one the most adult occasions of western visual art, the observed appearance of an object successfully provided an aesthetic mode. The *Tempesta* contains none of the tension of conceptual art nor yet a minute chasing of detail uncharged with a general poetry. An immanence is there while the whole is relaxed.

Any contemplation of the visual world is a scanning of the soul. Where contemplation is properly aesthetic there is no "mystic" reading into Nature. The fantasies evoked by texture and chromatic interchange, purely aesthetic matters, expressed in terms of the senses, can provide an immediate yet profound commentary upon life. Giorgione's art is not the expression of a philosophical or mystical idea. On the contrary, by imbuing objects and their relation with aesthetic value he created a philosophy which I have affirmed to be relevant today.

Turner: beneficence in space [iii]

There is a long history of indistinctness in Turner's art, connected throughout with what I have called an embracing or enveloping quality, not least of the spectator with the picture. The power grew in Turner of isolating the visionary effectiveness that belongs to a passing event of light: it entailed some loss of definition in the interest of emphasis upon an overall quality. To one who complained,

---

iii   From "The art of Turner", *Painting and the Inner World*, 1963, pp. 50, 59-60, 63-69, 73-78; *Critical Writings* III, pp. 237, 242-243, 245-249, 252-255.

Turner is said to have replied: "Indistinctness is my forte."

[...]

If the deepest aim was transcendent, Turner employed for it his vast experience of measure. There is small appearance of the arbitrary in his drifts of mountain, sea and sky: they formulate an erratic architecture or a superb natural habitat, no less than an irresistible phenomenon; soft and tenuous, warmed as well as cold. It was as if catastrophes were carvings on the sky: they stem from the delicate use of the pencil in thousands of drawings, slight touches to enrich the paper as if it were a volume invoked by this touch, remarkable not only for delicacy but for selectiveness, even in so early an architectural drawing as the sketch of Stamford, Lincolnshire, of 1797. Unity of treatment is matched by that of feeling: what is grasped from the subject is accorded with the projected strain of feeling that encompasses and adjusts each detail with another.

[...]

A price had to be paid for the homogeneous effect, a price on which Turner's critics were agreed; not only that: his flattening of figures and tempering of foreground in the interest of overall effect corresponded to a lack of inevitable interest in relief, shown by the playing down of figures as a result of his growing concentration upon the enveloping landscape. We shall find that these attitudes are possibly linked in deeper layers of the mind also. On the other hand, early studies of buildings, hills, and especially rocks, are often very notable for their relief. Turner was a phenomenal draughtsman in several genres, but particularly for choice and disposition of accent and bare space in a finely controlled sea of detail; for a pointilliste employment as a youth, in company with Girtin, of the pencil's point within a pattern of short strokes. His drawings of the figure at the Academy schools were no more than adequate. Some later drawings of the nude are considerably better, but do not obtain high significance. Except in the case of cows and of the early self-portrait in oil, his delineation of faces seems wooden. We cannot discover in Turner's art much affirmative relationship to the whole body, to human beings. They tend to be sticks, or fish that bob or flop or are stuffed. The prejudice is sometimes allowed such freedom, that many figures who should be dignified appear to be rustic, to be approached by the artist with unconcealed because untutored naivety, though this is in fact very far from the case. To use the psychoanalytic term, they suggest part-objects. (A part-object, it may be recalled, is an organ or function that on the analogy of the first object, the breast, has been split off from an object's other organs and functions: a part-object, therefore, is a concept at a great distance from the one of a whole, separate person for whom, in a regression, it may come to stand).

[...]

I must recall that the relationship to a part-object has the character of a complete identification, of a whirlpool envelopment into which we are drawn. Of such kind is Turner's more usual conception of doom and disaster [...], the conception, in one aspect, of the infant who believes in the omnipotent and scalding propensity that belongs to his stream of yellow urine as it envelops the object so closely attached to himself, an object split off in his mind from the good breast with which he is also one. Whereas the two trends are integrated in Turner's art, he must emphasize with less vigour the long-studied separateness of self-sufficient and whole objects, other than as the pictures themselves, with a viewpoint, maybe, from above, now removed from the artist. The overall emphasis upon the canvas is predominantly the one of envelopment. We are likely to think first of late Turners in this connection. Though the approach be traditional the same quality is rarely absent from any but the earliest drawing and watercolour sketches.

[...]

After considerable and continuous success as a very young man, Turner's first great triumph was in 1801 with the Bridgewater sea piece; already in 1802 (elected R. A.) he is accused of lack of finish; later, it will be of offering his public mere blotches. These, as a matter of fact, he kept to himself. In some cases, attributable mostly to the years 1820-30, of what Finberg in his Turner Bequest catalogue calls "Colour beginnings" watercolours (especially T. B. 263; there are also uncatalogued oil sketches), one is aware of experimentation with paint, yet of discoveries sufficient to themselves, though they can often be read without difficulty as first sketches in colour of landscapes and seascapes or as records of natural effects for which his memory was phenomenal.

But it is impossible at this point, the crux of the Turner enigma, to remove his technical and aesthetic probing, probings into landscape design, from pressures anterior to them. All obsession has a vivid aspect of self-sufficiency. Anyone who looks through items, other than the earliest, of the vast Turner Bequest, will be amazed at the number of these "beginnings" and pencil sketches, often monotonous in simplicity and sameness in regard to a raining downward of a top area upon a receptive area below; so many sheets in later times have no other feature, while others have a reverse surge from the lower section made up of vibrant stripes parallel to the picture plane, or of piercing forms as from an uneven sea. It appears that with the latter years, Turner brushed in large oil paintings for exhibition upon such preparations, sometimes their entirety as representations during the varnishing days. One element assaults the other in the simple, zoned beginnings. Concentrating upon sky with land or sea, the artist was under compulsion to record faithfully and repeatedly a stark intercourse, then to reconcile, then to interpose, perhaps with a rainbow. Among the "Studies for vignettes" of the 1830s (T. B. 280) there is a watercolour sheet of rose with touches of ochre, saturated at the bottom, thin above. Underneath this apparently abstract design of melting colour, Turner has written – so runs the guess – "Sauve qui peut". It is to be expected that such delicate interplay of two colours enfolded already for him the terrors of a flood, equal to the chromatic balm in virtue of which the inevitable alternation of the terror could be allowed to appear.

With comparable obsessiveness in his middle and final years, Turner would draw rapidly a tower ensconced on a hill-top, over and over again from every angle, perhaps six linedrawings on one small page, doubtless with an eye to the best design for a painting, but also to make far more than certain from every long approach how the one element fitted into the other: he often drew next day another tower and hill-top with this fervour. An approximation, a drawing together, the forging of an identity, so to say, out of evident differences as is revealed by a fine use of colour, was a constant aim. In his catalogue Finberg wrote of sketch-book 281 in the Turner Bequest: "A number of these pages have been prepared with smudges of red and black water-colour, the colour then being dabbed and rubbed, with the object apparently of producing suggestions of figures, groups etc." Maybe, but no figure or group suggestions are to be seen, only the reconciliation of the dense with the less dense. They resemble another common type of beginning that is diapha-nous and equal throughout. For, naturally, rather than a prime imposition of contrast, some coloured beginnings pre-eminently possess, like lay-ins, the opposite or complementary value, that of the carver's elicitation upon the stone's surface of a prevalent form attributed to the block. Turner often used a rough blue or grey paper on which his panoramic pencil drawings (even more than watercolouring) suggest messages that have appeared from within a wall upon its surface. An eloquent surface in this sense was integral to his art and became increasingly an influence upon its content. Divorced from that bent, his flamboyant confronta-tions would have lacked their union, the ease of interchange and coalescence, the issue of light, so often sunset, that floods.

In a region of the mind, as I have indicated, properties of fire and water (scalding) are not at variance but united, the hose of the fireman with the fire he inflames and, indeed, initiates. "All his life," wrote Kenneth Clark of Turner in passages to which I am much indebted, "he had been obsessed by the conjunction of fire and water." And: "He loved the brilliance of steam, the dark diagonal of smoke blowing out of a tall chimney and the suggestion of hidden furnaces made visible at the mouth of a funnel." Earlier, in *Landscape into Art*, Clark had a heading: "Fire in the Flood", a quotation from *Beowulf*. "Throughout the landscape of fantasy", he wrote, "it remains the painter's most powerful weapon, culminating in its glorious but extrava-gant use by Turner." I think he enlarged upon fire in the flood far beyond this context of a Nature that was feared on every

side in a dark and insecure age; it was a fear that must always
have existed everywhere for irrational reasons alone, since there
are bound to be phantasies of revengeful attacks issuing in kind
from a scalded mother. Turner, it seems to me, largely denied this
fear, pursued the attack but accepted the doom: he was possibly
eager to discover those phantasies "acted out" by a happening
that he could represent as realism. In January 1792, when he
was sixteen, he soon visited the burnt-out Pantheon in Oxford
Street. A feature of his watercolour of the site next morning are
icicles clinging to the façade, frozen water from the hoses. (In
late life he attended to the processes of whaling – one instance is
the boiling of blubber while the boats are entangled by a flaw
ice – and, of course, to giant sea-monsters). It is the first occasion
of which we know that Turner's pencil, to use an expression of
the time, was employed upon smouldering disaster. He was on
the scene when the Houses of Parliament were burning in 1834;
he made watercolour sketches and then two oil paintings; the
sketches are among his great masterpieces. Flames enwrap the
highways of the sky and of the Thames. Vessels coaling by torch-
light, *Keelmen Heaving in Coals by Night*, is another lurid canvas
of this period. When he returned to Venice, probably in 1835,
he painted several sketches of rockets fired from ships during a
fiesta. A criticism of his *Juliet and Nurse*, executed on his return,
in which fireworks figure, was to the effect that he made the
night sky far too light. Another writer said that *Juliet and Nurse*
was nothing more than a further conflagration of the Houses
of Parliament. Turner exhibited in 1832 *Nebuchadnezzar at the
Mouth of the Fiery Furnace.* "Fire" or "heat" and "blood" were
words commonly used in contemporary writing on him. It is
surely unnecessary to remark, in respect to fire and water, the
many watery sunrises and bloody sunsets or *Rain, Steam and
Speed* and *Fire at Sea*. Turner himself wrote "Fire and Blood" in
the sky of a drawing that may be dated 1806–8 (T. B. 101). The
onrush of ivy and other leafage in his best architectural drawings
are profoundly related with effects of rock and water such as
the wonderful watercolour of 1795, *Melincourt Fall,* where the
unbroken slab or wedge of water licks the fractured rock like a

flame. Soon after reaching Rome for the first time in October 1819, Turner hurried to Naples where Vesuvius had become active some days before.

Allied with the one of fire there is often conveyed by his work a sense of explosion, in the famous *Snowstorm* (exhibited 1842), for instance, or even in the earlier snowstorm of *Hannibal Crossing the Alps* of 1812. One sees from afar an atmosphere of paint and detonation, then one searches for the benighted human beings who, when found, remark the processes of meteorological might rather than of individuals who endure them. On the other hand, Olympic vistas, calm temples, survive in our general impression of Turner's art: in view of a ceaseless lyrical bias it is a humane art. We learn from him that calamity is asymmetrical.

Ruskin deplored Turner's lack of interest in the detail of Gothic architecture (despite the numerous, astounding studies of, say, Rouen cathedral). A brooding attachment to the classical orders is strangely suggested by bawdy lines he wrote eroticizing the Ionic. (It is not altogether surprising to discover there a punning use of words that could reflect the infantile oral phantasy of the *vagina dentata*.)

In connection with my mention of scalding attacks I think it relevant to remark Turner's liberal use of yellows. Dido building Carthage was originally thought too yellow. Turner himself writes to a friend in 1826: "I must not say yellow, for I have taken it all to my keeping this year, so they say." And later that year: "Callcott is going to be married to an acquaintance of mine when in Italy, a very agreeable Blue Stocking, so I must wear the yellow stockings." Rippingille reported from Rome a *mot* about a retailer of English mustard who was coupled with Turner: "The one sold mustard, the other painted it." "A devil of a lot of chrome" is how Scarlett Davis described to Ince the *Burning of the House of Lords and Commons*. (Van Gogh, a more aggressive handler of everything fiery, and his passion for yellow, are better known today.)

I find it fair to say that the compulsively unitary, forcing side of Turner's art strengthened, indeed largely inspired, a further linking by his late paintings of elements already long harmonized through the delicacy of his touch, through his heightened sense of texture and colour relationship, a building, for instance, and its foliage, the structure and its attenuations, what is rough with what is smooth, the perpendicular with the transverse by means of the ellipse. I have emphasized primitive and aggressive compulsions in Turner's art, but I have wanted to suggest that in admitting them, in giving due place to ferocity and the consequent despair, his very powerful lyrical vein was not impaired; throughout his oeuvre it was enriched; in many, very many, supremely lyrical works, a linking, a co-ordination, an integration, of different degrees of compulsion and different tendencies of the mind were achieved. In the great last period, not only is the world washed clean by light, but humidity is sucked from water, the core of fire from flame, leaving an iridescence through which we witness an object's ceremonious identity: whereupon space and light envelop them and us, cement the world under the aegis of a boat at dawn between Cumaean headlands, or a yacht that gains the coast.

Together with Turner's whirlpool of fire and water we experience beneficence in space. There abound calm scenes that would be sombre or forlorn without the gold, without the agitated pulse and delicacy in so light a key.

Beneficence is very widely scattered; encompasses from afar.

(64-69; 245-249)

[...]

I must enlarge upon clefts and clumps before referring to the counterpoint. If these be allegories of feminine form and function as a whole, yet the nuzzling, the enveloping, the part-object symbolism, is their stronger facet, so often dramatized in representations of vast space, by Turner's own small figure also, in top-hat and tail-coat (*vide* the Parrott portrait) with nose almost pressing it as he works a considerable canvas at the Academy or British Institution, without stepping back. Though it is written by an artist who was usually hostile and malevolent about Turner, some of the account, confirmed in the main elsewhere, is worth remark of Turner and his *Burning of the House of Lords and Commons* on a varnishing day, 1835, at the British Institution.

"He was there at work", wrote E. V. Rippingille in a reminiscence of Callcott (*Art Journal*, 1860) "before I came, having set to work at the earliest hour allowed. Indeed it was quite necessary to make the best of his time, as the picture when sent in was a mere dab of several colours, and "without form and void" (Hazlitt), like chaos before the creation." Etty was working at his side, on his picture *The Lute Player*:

> Little Etty stepped back every now and then to look at the effect of his picture lolling his head on one side and half-closing his eyes, and sometimes speaking to someone near him, after the approved manner of painters: but not so Turner; for the three hours I was there – and I understood it had been the same since he began in the morning – he never ceased to work, or even once looked or turned from the wall on which his picture hung. All lookers-on were amused by the figure Turner exhibited in himself, and the process he was pursuing with his picture . . . Leaning forward and sideways over to the the right, the left-hand metal button of his blue coat rose six inches higher than the right, and his head buried in his shoulders and held down, presented an aspect curious to all beholders . . . Presently the work was finished: Turner gathered up his tools together, put them into and shut up the box, and then, with his face still turned to the wall, and at the same distance from it, went sideling off, without speaking a word to anybody.

We can take it that in the act of painting, even his vast distances were pressed up against the visionary eye like the breast upon the mouth: at the same time it was he who fed the infant picture. In these embracing conceptions, no wonder that figures glue themselves on banks and bases, variegated figures, salmon-like, dully flashing films of colour, perhaps floating beneath a cloud-like architecture, perhaps pressed to the ground like the catch in baskets upon a quay, glistening at dawn. Ruskin remarked on the accumulations of bric-a-brac in Turnerian foregrounds – I would include bodies and jetsam in seas, or on an earth so flattened in some late canvases as to suggest a pavement of rippled water – and referred them to the grand confusion of Covent Garden where Turner lived as a child. An equation persists, as is well known, between nipple and phallus. The above description of Turner at work in 1835 at the British Institution may recall the couplet twice used in his incomprehensible verses entitled "The origin of vermilion" or "The loves of painting and music":

> As snails trail o'er the morning dew
> He thus the line of beauty drew.

He sought daring expedients for his sense of fitness: in the case of persons especially, I repeat, they were based on part-object models. The companions, the siblings, he projected, are often like shoals; as mere members, as mouths perhaps, they may flit about the declivities and rises of an encompassing breast, much of it out of reach as palace, torrent, ocean, mountain or murderous sky.

No wonder Turner criticized Poussin's *Deluge* in the Louvre for lack of "current and ebullition" in the water, though he was much influenced by Poussin at that time (1802). Ruskin wrote as follows for the first volume of *Modern Painters* about *The Slave Ship*: "The whole surface of the sea is divided into two ridges of enormous swell, not high, not local, but a low broad heaving of the whole ocean, like the lifting of its bosom by deep-drawn breath after the torture of the storm."

These are mounds, clumps, of terror and benignity; within one of the shapes, a pyramid of pearly monsters has been confounded with the black, disappearing bodies. The pyramid of *Fire at Sea*, huge, massive, is thrown upwards against a mound of cloud. Swart, irregular pyramids characterize the famous *Snowstorm* whose ship is like a broken caterpillar, whereas the engulfed mariners of *Fire at Sea* are near to having become, as if protectively, globular, saffron-coloured fish. A subject for Turner's attention, particularly in the neighbourhood of Plymouth during 1811, as numerous drawings and two canvases at Petworth testify, lay with the tall curving ribs of naval hulks, ruined globes of timber, derelict hills that rode upon the Tamar. The *Téméraire* would later achieve amid sunset fires superb apotheosis for hulks, unruined, full of distance from the funnelled infant steamboat by which it is tugged, to which it is closely attached.

It would be tedious to enumerate the recurrence of a fluidity that possesses clumps, mounds, pyramids and clefts, though I am fascinated by this theme, especially in paintings that Turner showed at his last Academy of 1850, *Visit to the Tomb* and *Departure of the Trojan Fleet*, among his ultimate Punic paintings. I must remark the extraordinary volume of such unmoored shapes, since there was earlier mention of poorness of relief in another context. Had he been primarily a figure painter – in this matter it is no contradiction to imagine so – Turner would have attained poignant compositions in terms of that theme: the so-called *Costume Piece* at the Tate suggests it.

To summarize Turner's clump or mound conception would be, I think, to isolate a parting of the ways, a rustling or seething withdrawal as in the biblical passage of the Red Sea: to many mythological scenes an opalescent, warm passage is common through the centre, and on one side, maybe, the silent arm of a tall pine.

It remains to speak of the tension, the counterpoint, the bringing together of storm with sun, disaster with beauty, melancholy with protected ease in many, many, parkland expanses, and, in general, the good with the bad. Formal contrivances that suggest their union are not of course themselves symbolic in the immediate conscious sense of the rainbow, for instance, of *The Wreck Buoy*. More significant, however, even here (as deep-laid symbol), the high, lit, sail-tops, ghostly against a sky that falls in curtains of rain, cleave to the rainbow's half-circle triangularly, in contrast with fore-ground water, wastes rich in light flanked by darker mounds of sea, that topple over towards the spectator yet seem at the back to climb up to the boats and to the falling sky. The meeting of these movements occurs near the centre of the canvas from where one has the sense of extracting the heart of so vertiginous, so desert, yet so various a scene, in terms of the red-rose jib on the nearer sailing boat: at either side verticals incline outwards and thereby stress that centre. Awareness of a centre in great space will favour a rencontre of contrary factors in whatever sense.

Turner was no stranger to the manipulation and perhaps even to the confusion of contrary factors. I cannot help remarking, as shown to me by B. A. R. Carter, that two demonstration sheets, illustrating a triangle fitted into a circle, that he used for his Perspective lectures, are each headed "Circle (or circles) within a triangle".

A motif more constant in the work of Turner even than the one of clumps with their clefts, is the rhythmic use of a rebuttal, very commonly of waves blown back as they break on a lea shore, apparent already in early sea pieces and in mountain brooks whose drums of shallow water rolling over boulders provide the effect of a reversing power, a break. He often represents the force of natural agency by demonstrating that it is engaged, sometimes thwarted by another. *The Falls of Terni* drop as one body, then are broken, buffetted. A stoic pathos, inherent in the beauty, sustains those great last light canvases wherein hardly a boat interrupts the grappling of sea with sky, wherein naked oppositions and their reconciliation supply overall bareness to the opulence of the effect. Yet even in narrow paintings of flat scenes, *Chichester Canal* or *Petworth Park with Tillington Church in the Distance* (sketches at the Tate for the Petworth landscapes), at the meeting of ground and sky there is the effect of a scooped-out pomegranate or apricot common to the pictures of Petworth interiors, a benign application of the whirlwind principle, at the picture's centre, at the centre of interest. (The theme is at least as old as exquisite studies for *The Sun Rising through Vapour.*) Maybe a low sun is there to help us seize upon the otherwise faintly indicated fruit, both soft and fierce, romantic in promise as in muted danger and elusive distance. Amid the embraces of hugeness, we have seen that figuration, men more than cattle, are sometimes a startling variant, like fossil traces that vivify a rock. The infant's experiences have been similarly engraved by him upon the sudden breast.

Clasping natural immensity, Turner lent a hard-won grandeur to the distance, so irregularly spanned by each of us, between self-destruction and forgetful, infantile love.

As he elaborates an insight conditioned by his time, the artist, I have supposed in the first essay ["Painting and the inner world"], may project images that need not correspond altogether with his most native bent. Naturally, the correspondence will have been very close in the case of superb individualists. All the same, it is impossible even to guess how potently Turner's uniqueness could have survived abstraction from the historical context, and it is impossible to know how deeply, how widely, the primitive obsessions that were exploited by his art, qualified the structure of his ego. In making an end, therefore, not only to this brief examination of his peculiar genius but also to wider issues in this book, a word or two are required for the other side of the balance.

A broad issue has been the artist's ambivalence, the bringing together he imposes on it. Turner pre-eminently dramatized that *rencontre* when he applied it to a state where it does not truly belong, to the earlier emotions of overpowering alternations before ambivalence has been admitted, embracing the then current notions of "the sublime", of what is rapturous, transporting yet often vast and terrible, in a word, enveloping. Through chromatic wealth, through the brilliant identity between great differences that colour can create, an equation habitually survives in Turner's major work between dissolution, disruption and suave continuity, between richness and the bareness of distance: neither term suffers from their union; neither is overlaid, disguised. While light that dominates so many of his landscapes is rich and bounteous, it obliterates also, flooding building, water and mountain to the length, sometimes, of their near-extinction. Accepting his sublimity, entertaining thus a merging experience, the spectator shrinks as a complete or separate entity but regains himself as he absorbs the stable self-inclusiveness of the art object.

CHAPTER SIX

Construction of the good mother

Inside out: *an autobiographical narrative* [i]

This is not a book about childhood, except for a little of my own. The "working-out", as the title suggests, a certain relation to the external world, provides the subject.

(From the preface to *Inside Out,* 1947)

Going down the hill one morning towards Lancaster Gate, my eldest brother remarked on an orange cloud in a dark sky: a thundercloud, he said. And sure enough, that afternoon there was a thunderstorm. At nearby Stanhope Gate, an old woman sold coloured balloons. It was as if the lot had burst. I think I remember well this small event since it symbolizes an exceptional happening. For once the glowering suspense, the feeling of things hardly redeemed, was contradicted by a menace that came to violent fruition. The thing was done and finished with: the storm happened and passed, and the small orange

i From *Inside Out,* 1947, 7-32; *Critical Writings* II, 142-158.

cloud had shown it was to happen. None of the other omens I can remember was either read or fulfilled as was this. The year would be 1908 or so, when I was six.

I used to single out the cars in the processional traffic on the road round the park, and count them. Their cautious, noisy explorations without an objective, without an arrival point, a trundling round the park, helped to create the atmosphere of grinding suspense. Meanwhile, beyond the cruel railings, the scarlet horse-buses with Tatcho advertisements roared down Bayswater Road. The railings were cruel, I think, because of the tramps who sat on seats outside, in waste-paper and drowsy filth: and whatever was railed within the park, suggested a burning-cold, a searing prohibition against those who would slink away into the iron ivyness of copse or plantation. Other single railings were isolated in the open parts of the park. Their usefulness would seem to be confined to that of a threat against the couples who blundered in the dark, choosing an exposed and therefore isolated place in which to lie. There seemed to be no love in that love-making. To the small boy, the immersed, in-rolled couple suffered from a still greater poverty than did the single drunks who slumbered face to the sky. The evil was poverty, not crime or drink. Poverty itself was destructive. Dirt, smell and the bleary eye, all to my mind, smart and noisome activities, were the predominant performances of poverty.

I was forbidden to sit on the seats with complicated cast-iron sides frequented by the destitute. Nevertheless, regarding these seats as forlorn homes, I was fascinated, not only by the danger imputed to them, an infection, as it were, of poverty, but by the possibility of constant acts of restitution. I would therefore implore my governess, in spite of the ban, to use these seats; and I would get behind, between the low railing at the side of the walk and the back of the seat, and imagine that I was making this last refuge, for all the bareness of board and of cold, jarring contortion of cast-iron, to "work", whether as a ship or car or whatever purposeful vessel took my fancy.

The *underneath* of the seat, at any rate, was my discovery, this space between the seat and the low rail in front of the grass, almost roofed by the sloping of the seat's back. Those who had forbidden it, had not examined that side. Could I keep the underneath alive and thus cause the animation of the whole?

This occasional game helped me very little to endow the park and its inhabitants with health. There were vaster engines than my seat which I could not control. The machine house of the fountains, for instance, had an ominous air. A scour of mysterious steam hung over a sunken tank at the back of the engine house and was appre-hended at the same time as the smell of oil and the clanking of the lethal cylinders. The cold and grinding mechanism was housed in Portland stone of a late Victorian style, both white and darkened. The fountains themselves had little grace owing to the pretentiousness of every detail of the stone layout. Moreover, the smell of decay was freshened by the sprayed water that dropped like pellets on the surfaces of the basins. Surplus water from the final basin poured away into the Long Water. Here was the inky-dark medium of the park suicides. My governess and I used to read outside the park police station the notices recounting, in the hope of further information which brought a reward (printed in large letters), all the crimes that had recently occurred, chiefly suicides in the Serpentine. A police description of a dead body exactly expressed my predominant impres-sion of the park as a whole. Yet I did not altogether give up hope of infusing these remnants with life. I would return again and again to the fountains and hope against hope that the engine-house activity would spell out something good. It was indeed worse when, as so often, the fountains were not working and the water licked the lichened sides more blackly without the bombardment of pellets. To see the fountains turned on – as I often did – was a fine sight, since the spouts grew from a trickle to an inch, to a foot, to a yard, finally reaching a great height, sustained there by an eager, pumping pulse: at the summit, rainbow colours could be discerned; a thin elegant summit sometimes torn by the wind but formed again immediately. The wind might tear off the whole summit or bend the column like a tree, but the compensating power returned in the end. This entirely mechanical restitution did not please me: the power behind it was blind, exact and faithless in the sense that it did not deal in faith. Perhaps, indeed, the relentless mounting of the fountains when they were turned on, propelled by each stroke of the very extensive engine, was really most frightening to me.

The fountains played. Dirty children rushed from basin to basin: suspicious park-keepers stalked their antics, generally from afar. The keepers had boxes scattered in the park, so that their emergence could have something of the suddenness associated with the paratroop whose landing has not been observed. The keepers carried whistles. Emergence from a telephone booth is always associated by me with the fingering of something tucked away on one side of the chest, a cold, punishing little organ that it was a positive duty to handle. When a park whistle was blown near the fountains, the shrill sound seemed to travel on an eagle journey, piercing the water pellets whose clattering was considerable. In fact, you had to shout to make yourself heard near the fountains.

We called the elderly ragamuffins and tramps of the park "parkees". I had wandered away from my nurse who was chatting on the walk above the fountains. Among the basins I was seized by a pack of parkees and my shouts could not be heard even a few feet away. I managed to break loose – I had the wooden handle of a push-cart with me – and regained the nurse who had noticed nothing. In spite of my remembrance, I have little doubt that no such actual thing happened. Probably the context existed; parkees spoke to me and I had been warned against such intercourse by having the fear of being kidnapped instilled in me. But a kind of feud was invented. When the nurses and their children congregated, I would glance across at the other encampment of mothers and poor children and tramp women who seemed to watch every straying movement: and perhaps, wellarmed with a stick, I would run half-way in their direction, testing the evil in comparative safety.

Sometimes the positions of the opposing camps would be reversed. We would be in the fountains, and the less intent parkees (since they always inhabited these seats) would be the objects of apprehension as they sat on a stone seat with a curious round termination on the walk above, or in the high, disproportionate alcove on the hill, down from Victoria Gate.

The tall, disproportionate alcove, shallow, high and cold, with toddlers squirming on a low brown seat, was, and is today (though it be attributed to Wren), an image to me of blindness. This kind of ethical ugliness in the use of a classical form, particularly the cruel denial of shadow or depth in proportion to the height, afflicted me to such an extent that I think it has helped me in later life to find good architecture to be a particular symbol of life. Nearly all the monuments and buildings in the park, including the fountains, professed for me the same cruel discrimination.

It was little better with the forms of life abounding on the lake, or with the dogs allowed to race and bounce about for a liverish hour, or led to lamp-post or rail on a lead. Obscenely different in size, they fought each other, raced and wrestled. In conjunction with the drawing-room salutations of their owners, their curiosity about each other appeared particularly morbid. The animal world seemed a sheer importation, a waywardness controlled with distaste and severity.

It was the same with the birds, largely fed by hand. An old man would be feeding sparrows. Their hopping and twittering and mass scurries of flight seemed to express his own accumulated evasions.

There were the peacocks which could be watched between the bars of the railings at the side of the Long Water. These disconsolate birds would sometimes spread a tail. A keeper fed them and to him was attributed all the powers of their control.

Yet occasionally, at times of post-luncheon winter sunsets, there was an atmosphere of Nature in the park. Smoke from bonfires and a decreasing light suggested some limit to control, and the yelling of peacocks from a nook surprisingly distant, dislodged for a time an imputed curriculum.

Nevertheless, the ducks and other water-fowl seemed no less chained than the sparrows upon the neat paths. There are two gaps by the side of the Long Water, where the railings and concealing shrubbery cease, where the path comes to the edge of the water. In these two small bays the ducks are visited and fed. Even here, there is a kind of fencing, though it is in the water. The ducks enter through gaps. The shore is edged by a sloping stone kerb. A thin line of scum, feathers, soot, twigs, laves the lower edge of the rough stones which above are wetted by the slitherings of those ducks who land to be fed. Sometimes, too, there is a collection of geese with pincushion foreheads, needle eyes and evident ill-temper. The easy floating of the birds on water causes the uneasy trundling and shooting necks of the birds ashore to appear painful. The swans particularly look broad and gross in this shore wrangling for crumbs. The eyes of all the birds seem to pierce their heads as the keepers' whistles pierce the fountains' spray. They have their home upon an island in the Serpentine where at night they may be self-governing, though watched, as it were, by the monotonous sentry duty of the traffic in Knightsbridge.

The swans I knew to be fierce. There were stories of a blow from a wing smashing a man's leg and of the uselessness of an opened umbrella as a guard. Sometimes they moved on the water with ruffled plumage. Once, in minatory Edwardian stateliness, a swan was seen sitting on a nest below the fountains, just to the side of the dangerous overflow from the fountains into the Long Water, a miniature eddying waterfall whose downward suction or pull was challenged, but not refuted, by the even keel of the giant bird sitting on her dry nest.

Just as in the case of the parkees, when I was older and able to row a boat I used to come as close as I dared to this waterfall-termination of the Long Water. The flow, in fact, was small. But the dangers of the park as a whole could not thus be disproved.

Where did the water go? At the other end of the lake there was a low white bridge whose several arches were perhaps not more than a foot above the level of the water. Did the water flow away here where, even a swimmer, still less a boat, could not penetrate the mystery? This white stone bridge had a certain grace: the exceedingly low arches, however, were associated in my mind with a challenge to any inquisitive and anxious head whether of water fowl or man, who tried to share the fate, whatever it might be, of the water beyond the Serpentine.

On the further side of the white bridge there was a sharp declivity and a high though meager waterfall. I don't think that I connected this water with a flow from the Serpentine. Later, I was to hear that most of the Serpentine water passed underground and came up in the park of Buckingham Palace. I was to be told that the Serpentine could be drained, that everything flung into it could be brought to light. All the miseries of the torn, attacked and divided mother without me and within, she who was the park and all that happened there, to be known, controlled and restored? No wonder that in many later enquiries I have sought for the clean sweep. I have had an absurd faith in the efficacy of generalization and, at times, a neurotic subservience to the behests of an apparent logic. By this would-be control I have been subservient to the same relentless animus that informed, to my mind, the face of the park.

The park, of course, was not the first desolation but it is the one I remember first, the setting down in the external world of the sum of earlier desolations. Nature, in man and beast and flower, was a thing chained and divided. It would seem that each blade of grass, smelling of London even when it grew rankest, could be examined. There were no weeds. Sheep left droppings on the grass, left them there, so it appeared, just as towards sunset some living bundle of rags would seem to be left forlorn on a green chair for the use of which a penny should have been paid. It was not usual for us to sit on these chairs. If we did, often the ticket collector would come unseen from behind us, cutting across the grass with a town gait, with his roll of tickets and his clippers moving loosely in front of him like a sporran. This ship of the park was another examining agent.

Banked-up by gardeners, flowers were viewed through railings, a splendent array in spring near Victoria Gate, just in front of the dogs' cemetery of which you could obtain one glance from the top of a bus bound for Queen's Road. Between you and the military rows of flowers was a wide grass verge and a high railing. Nearby there was a rustic cottage. In the course of time I grew very curious concerning this and other cottages, and a well-sized house in the middle of Kensington Gardens. I had never seen anyone go in or come out, but most delicious wood smoke was often climbing from the chimneys. These cottages and their small enclosed gardens, far more than the park grass or the trees or the flowers, suggested to me the open country, unknown to me except for the landscapes I saw from the train window on the way to the seaside. Later I used to imagine myself inhabiting the house in the middle of Kensington Gardens; walking the park in the early morning, watching the dawn and later seeing the lines of trees, an unspoilt natural panorama; living in the country in the middle of London. From adolescence onwards I did what I could with my imagination to restore the park. Standing at the Round Pond, I looked across the Long Water and conjured up the vista of an eighteenth-century park, a royal park having no essential connection with the lives of children.

But it was dust-laden; every blade of grass was discerned for a metropolitan purpose. The sheep would leave wool on trees, a dubious trail in a well-known spot on all sides of which London traffic roared. In summer there was the clipping and a branding and a dip, down near the police station. The startled shorn bodies suggested a touch of extreme "nature", a nakedness, an exhibitionism, even, a sudden production of the pale body, a child's amorous game, a suicide, a thousand little boys running nude into the Serpentine on a hot summer evening, allied somehow with the world of correctitude, railings and park-keepers; with parkees and violent dirt, no less.

And so, the candles of the beautiful chestnut trees were sullied and dangerous in my eyes. Only the countless blossom of the may trees with their sweet dusty town smell, seemed poised and without potential disaster. In a polite and a young form the bloom of these trees was the microcosm of the continent of endless brick where hope lay among the clustered varied chimney pots. I remember picnics under the may trees near Victoria Gate: I remember the brown osier lunch basket with osier pin like a giant hat pin, and the contents spread on the tame grass. Two older girls with their nurses used to join our party of three brothers and a nurse. Sylvia had a reddish face and Enid was pale, with freckles, green eyes and long legs. A saga about parkees was begun at those picnics. Heat glittered beyond the tossed-up may trees in flower: between the trees traffic glinted, seen from the eye-level of the grass. This circular flow of traffic served as a kind of watchful coasting on the fringes of consciousness: at times, also, as vehicles which carried correspondence to the deeper depths of the mind, bringing thence the matter for new affinities. And yet this upward, as it were, and downward movement was expressed by a steady low-lying motion along a flat surface. There is pleasure, there is life, when movement, particularly even movement in space, when the outward world at large takes for us the form of the jagged, shifting promontories of the mind. It is notable, however, that the first glimpse of the sea, that closer parallel to the tossing mind, has a meaning of limitless release; and words wrested from a life at sea ring true of the mind.

As I walked at the side of the traffic from the bridge over the Serpentine to Victoria Gate, the extended movement of vehicles would express for me the hostile, unforgiving expanse of the sky. To the left there was rough ground with a deep ditch, the railed boundary between the park and Kensington Gardens. The rough ground just beyond the ditch epitomized the depth of frustration and hostility. It was here. I think, after my brothers had gone to school, that I tried to make casual friends by joining to kick a football. Also, at the end of this bit of ground, by the path going down to the fountains, I had confronted a little girl with a doll-like face called Helen who was the sister of a boy at my kindergarten. I longed to get to know her. I think there were rows and fights with possible friends on this piece of ground, the scene of failures in early attempts at sociability. For me, other children, like the rest of the furniture of the park, were objects of potential danger. Any difference in upbringing and in routine indicated a lost soul: for I was wrapt by the prohibitions and rituals in which I was educated and in terms of which I still hoped to make ultimate restitution. Projected on to the face of the park and there apprehended, the struggle was ugly, torn, stern, harrowed and dirtied, redeemed slightly – and here figured a half-concealment of the most profound anxiety – by a morbid melodrama.

I was a happy boy. By that I mean that both elders and contemporaries have told me that I gave them the impression of being happy, healthy, energetic. From my parents I had love and great care. There were occasional screaming fits, I am told, when I used to shout without end, "I want it all right".

What did I want put right? I had best say the park, since there is very little else that I remember either of the pleasure or the pain. The park I remember well.

I shall soon try to give a picture of the other side of this predominant state but in a subsequent form. I shall show how a good mother was finally constructed, in the external world as well as in myself. Art has played an important role. This is perhaps foreshadowed by my vain scrutiny of the monuments in the park: the giant Achilles statue at Hyde Park Corner, for instance, and, later, the Watts equestrian statue in the middle of the Long Walk. I had high hopes of the Watts because it was new; I remember it veiled and then unveiled. Such figures were to me stern yet impotent: figures of a father, then, who both attacked and had been attacked. These statues attempted to affront the sky yet they were recipients of fog, of bird droppings and of soot: they seemed unconnected with light. The Albert Memorial was of the category, with vain groupings and pseudo-sacred steps. Here was a great fuss about solid matter; here was a thing of arrest which, unlike the prohibiting railings, protested as well as forbade. It took many years for me to discover that art was not a kind of warning. What else was to be made of the sharp, pale, granite obelisk in the Long Walk, with the one word "Alma", with two steps and a platform edged by a decorous iron chain?

I think it might have been different if I had been allowed to approach Kensington Palace, the sunken Dutch garden and the Orangery. The only time I saw the Orangery, at the age of eight or nine, I was much impressed. For some reason, probably a fear of infection in an enclosed space, this part of the gardens was rigorously out-of-bounds. Perhaps because of this, still more because of the deep impression of the Orangery and its mild historic associations, the extreme limits of Kensington Gardens on the west side had magic for me: so much so, that I found it difficult to decide where were the exact limits. A sense of the infinite informed this very restricted space to the east of Kensington Park Gardens. The wall was high, but gardens stretched on the further side; termination came gently. In the shadow of that mysterious wall there lay a flat green where organized games were played of a different order from the haphazard kicking of a ball in the body of the park. I thought of this piece of ground as outside the park, yet at the same time, inside it, like a historical association pursued into the present. I was later to take great comfort in history, as if the things of the park, as if all that was carried inside my mind, could be pinned down, arranged, comprehended.

Meanwhile the traffic circulated without the park and within. All existed in suspense, and in pieces, yet stuck together. My suffering was at least magnified by the Edwardian centre of Empire.

The best epitome of massive, meticulous incoherence provided by the park was the Magazine at the end of the Serpentine Bridge. Explosive powder stood stored in this building of grey brick. A sentry always marched outside, and for all I know, does so to this day. Potential murder and death were guarded with careful pageantry. Except for the sentry's footfall there was a silence about the place, the seat of the greatest potential noise. Those stronger walls held the greater danger. I delighted in the sentry; I delighted in all soldiers. He was controlling the explosive powers within by his drilled movements.

What I remember most would seem to belong to autumn and winter. But singing of birds, in spring especially, the bursting buds on the trees, were not unnoticed: even a certain ecstasy in the air in early spring. The heart was not freed for long: the overlay of town smell and dirt, the very encouragement by the onlooker of pastoral things, denied them a reality that was supreme. Railings, decorous iron chains and park-keepers controlled such marionettes. I did not know the power of the earth. A row of hyacinths growing at Victoria Gate were "fixed" there by the authorities like the diminutive cockade in the top-hat of the coachman-like keeper of the Gate. And there was no horizon, no horizon at any time.

I associate Kensington Gardens most of all with years before I was six, Kensington Gardens rather than Hyde Park. From the time I was three until I was six, we had a very strict governess, a most patriotic Irish lady. If shoelaces came undone while out for a walk, there would be no jam for tea: if they again came undone, no cake either. This penalty fell particularly on my second elder brother to catch whom it was doubtless designed. I don't remember that it happened to me; nevertheless to this day I am extremely bad at improvising knots. After my brothers had gone to boarding school, Miss Drew was dismissed for maltreating me, so it is said, in the park. My mother has since told me that she had a letter from someone who witnessed the bad temper. I remember nothing about it: indeed, I remember little about Miss Drew except that she had a watch in the shape of a sword pinned to her breast, that she had moods of vivacity as well as of hot temper and that she painted pictures of battleships in moonlight.

After Miss Drew's time, the scene is more especially Hyde Park. My next caretaker was a Miss Harley, a morbidly religious middleaged woman. Miss Drew had also been religious, a Catholic. But now I was alone, without my brothers, as if the war were already starting and the Edwardian world were already crashing.

I had myself read in the Old Testament and had been deeply impressed by the effrontery shown by one side or the other in every issue, and by the venomous consequences. Miss Harley used to sing me hymns. She was for me the Salvation Army of morbid streets and morbid walks. Even the park sheep lo oked wicked and guilty, particularly the sheep, poor, smelly and sniffing. There was, I think, no talk of Christ. Perhaps it was forbidden since I was to be brought up as a simple theist at most. An essentially bachelor omnipresence, then, a bachelor blood-and-thunder, lay upon the slight hill beyond the Rotten Row, seared with paths like slow rolling tears of shame. He was a kind man – I understood that – this witness of all park lovemaking, sexual crimes and suicides, the magician among park-keepers as he proved himself to be in the garden of Eden or in speaking from bushes, or in hurling stone tablets out of the clouds. "Am I my brother's keeper?" Cain had said. That was a wicked, frightened joke of Cain's.

"Time like an ever-rolling stream, bears all her sons away." We used to sing that hymn, the thin sounds torn by the wind. I had never seen a rolling stream. I thought of it as the low thunder of the London traffic. And Time was the gloomy sky over the park, which, by turning into night, bore away the soiled fretfulness of all happenings there each day. The park monuments, then, especially the would-be works of art, possessed in my eyes an almost masochist quality in their utter poverty; impotent under the lash of Time, borne away each night to build their grimy ugliness anew each dawn. Between Marble Arch and Albion Gate there is a kind of Gothic steeple whose function is to provide several vents of drinking water. To this globuled monstrosity in particular I attributed a horrible masochism. There lingered no romance in its poverty nor in the poor frequenters; and as I was not allowed to drink such public water, I shunned it for being something blind and grey. Here stood no source, no spring . . . It is horrible that a flow of water, thin though the trickle, should come to represent a blindness.

But more than this. Except for that all-seeing eye, everything was blind, a skein of unseeing veins and sodden skin. Where were the eyes of those motorcars, those automobiles (under the crushed-down Renault bonnets?), those vehicles of Time itself? Vision, as well as Design, lay in the effortless sky alone.

I had the makings of a true and terrible fanatic for whom a single string of argument could trap the whole universe; I was later at one with the more inhuman speakers at Marble Arch. At another period every secret of the universe was contained for me on the walls of a big bookshop.

There were, however, rare moments when the purlieus known to me had stature. They were moments of pageantry preceded by weeks of preparation. 1910 was the year of Edward VII's funeral, 1911 of George V's coronation. I saw both processions. What stays in mind were the long thin festive poles swathed in scarlet cloth, tipped with golden spear-heads, that lined both sides of Bayswater Road. Even railings were tipped with gilt. It was not the gaudiness so much as the picking out of features, the slight rearrangement of the London forgetfulness, which gave the street a life to me. I saw, as it were, for the first time that Bayswater Road was a thorough-fare: some kind of plan appeared. But for a long time to come, apart from extreme religious fears especially for those I loved, I relied principally on the reading of history to reveal some connection in the surrounding scene.

The coronation brought soldiers to the park; thousands were encamped. A year or two before, Miss Harley had been succeeded by a Swiss, French-speaking governess, Mathilde. I think she must have been a fairly normal girl. She brought a homesick warmth. But the park held sway, and when we ate raspberry cream-filled chocolate bar which I had been forbidden, sitting in the park on one of the forbidden seats, my pleasure was not entirely sweet. I remember particularly some bedroom slippers on which had been spilt an extremely sticky spread which I liked, called Frame food jelly. This sweetness in the wrong place was agonizing. I used to wear those slippers because the nursery stood over my parents' bedroom and my father, at that time, lay fighting for his life although his imme-diate death had been prophesied by doctors who were crowding the house. Later, he was to watch in a dressing-gown through racing glasses, the distant passage of the King's funeral, seen in the distance from the balcony of the house.

Both Mathilde and I worshipped the soldiers. For a time I clung to military pomp and discipline as a "solution" of the park and its environs. In earlier years I had tried to order the universe by the arranging of lead soldiers. If one fell I was inconsolable.

And so, the face of the park came in part to be symbolized by a hybrid image of soldiers in scarlet jackets and by Marble Arch orators standing on soap-boxes. At this time, Mathilde and I sought the press of the crowd, in Rotten Row on a Sunday morning or around the bandstand of a summer evening. I have a pictorial, almost a Renoir-like, image – the only one of those times, based, I have little doubt, on much later experiences. For it is night, a dark, still night with rain in the air. The speakers at Marble Arch are lit with their torches; the outer fringe of whispering couples are lit by the lamps. Where it is dense the crowd is dark. Hats are in silhouette, so too the railings behind the speakers. Beyond, unwhispering grass is black except where a beam of light turns an outer fringe to emerald, the tired-smelling grass that otherwise would have been long obscured.

A soldier in a red tunic detaches himself from the crowd, takes the path across the park, probably making for Knightsbridge barracks. I watch him going between the far-flung lamps, making for the centre of the park and, so it seems, for the centre of the night since the park symbolizes all. I watch him go, getting less scarlet. Steadied by the lamps, my thoughts follow him into an immense space; for he has reached the open space where the enfolding pulse of the traffic is best felt. The lights, both near and distant, stare: an iron urge is to be attributed both to the soldier and to the preacher. Once and for all, I now put up the railings inside myself. I have an inspired feeling of Destiny, of Duty. I will follow out the most exacting inner imperative. With consistent dutiful fire I will equal the coldness and steadiness of the lamps; with a certain inner talisman I shall part the murmuring London sea; I shall prolong a selfless path with such resolution that the astonishing hideous pile of the Hyde Park hotel, so often figuring on the limits of vision, shall fall defeated below man's horizon . . .

Mathilde and I sought the crowds. Cross, genteel scents became familiar to me of a Sunday morning. The scene was shot with violent colour, of soldiers or perhaps of rhododendra. I think I attributed to these strong colours the power to strike, to hit out with the power of a dazzling wing.

We would often go to feed the ducks, either in the Long Water or in the Serpentine, taking bags of stale bread. I was aware of the possibilities of a certain ritual in the throwing of bread on the waters. The crumbs bobbed about and soaked; whereas the stale dry bread, particularly the brown, I found very appetizing. It made me hungry; I grudged the food to the ducks. However, in the feeding, the interest partly lay in trying to arrange for the ducks, or for any misguided bird on the outskirts, to have a share. Geese and baleful swans were the enemies. The ducks were defenceless and kindhearted, unmackintoshed mothers fed on sodden crumbs. Their surrounding water looked extremely desolate. Sparrows were at our feet, gulls in the air.

There was no haze of delight in this rapacious hunger. Finally, the empty bag having been burst, the paper was put to bob on the murky water in accordance with the wind. The walk home was marked by the passage underneath the Serpentine bridge. The dirty echoing tunnel with its lingering airs was cold at all times of the year. It was as if the passage lay beneath the dark water, here at its deepest according to a notice of warning. A dog would be barking like Cerberus. In view of the thunderous echoes, additional heads would have been in keeping.

I think to this obscene hole I attributed the home of the animus that tore the body of the park to shreds; the parkee spirit that made the park poor, hungry, desolate.

Each man invents a myriad states to counter his inferno. They exist abreast of the inferno; compensations, mitigations, transferences, controls, stern deletions, reparations. And so it has been with me. I have already referred to some of the priority repairs, as it were, by which an immediate patching up was attempted. But a truly exacting person, anxious to discover a reparation of even the smallest detail, is likely to construct a state parallel to that by which inferno is summed. And indeed, it is the initial imputation, in such a strong degree, of emotional states to the external world, inferno or paradiso or both at once; which characterizes the person who will primarily be an artist, even when childhood is passed. In this, however, I do not think he is peculiar, but only extreme and exacting in the use of an omnipotence commensurate with his anxiety.

Another tunnel, a long railway tunnel, the Mont Cenis, was the approach to the counter-landscape, to the rested mother, to love and life. This tunnel was the approach; not the centre of the landscape, but a symbol of rebirth.

On the near side of the tunnel there had been the Parisian evening, a wide glow, a width beyond what I knew. Then the rush through the night, the shriek of engines, like those of peacocks, through the ancient towns of Burgundy. They banished for me the engine cries of Victoria heard in Hyde Park, noises which at night had seemed deliberately to hollow an oblong trough of white upon the dark.

The Swiss mountains pointed a way in the morning. The pines too had the mountainous brow, the mountainous gesture, ranged in loftier and loftier perspective, many-armed as Siva, plated with snow.

I was prepared for Italy: I had been preparing from an early time. At the age of seven, in the years of Mathilde, I had gone to a day school. After a few terms, I started Latin grammar. I had learned from Mathilde a little French but my imagination had not been moved. I was fascinated immediately by Latin. I knew one word the first day mensa, a table-and how to decline it. I was fascinated, deeply stirred: I can remember the scene of that first lesson, where I sat, where the desks were, where the mantelpiece was. Not that I have any gift for languages; yet I possess the image of this declension of the word "mensa" on the first day of Latin, taught by a Miss Brown whom I liked. Of the table, for the table, by the table, each expressed by one simple word. The genitive case was the possessiveness of a simple love.

It is a scrubbed, sturdy, deal kitchen table, very bright: the fact that it is solid, that it stands on the floor is beautiful. The mensa table – or rather, a nexus of such experience, since it is most unlikely to have been in isolation – was a revolution in my life, an image the "feel" of which corresponds with an adult image of a simple table prepared for an al fresco meal, the family midday meal under a fig tree, with a fiasco of wine on the table, olives, a cheese and bread. With one word I possessed in embryo the Virgilian scene: a robust and gracious mother earth.

Although I continued to love Latin, and later Greek, until I came through the Mont Cenis, I did not repeat this experience so vividly.

Even as a small child I took particular note of barrel-organs, of their effect upon the neighbourhood. If their tunes were no substitute for the mensa experience yet somehow they had a connexion with it; an interest, it would seem, in another Italy, in the Baroque Italy.

From what I have attributed to the traffic in Hyde Park it will be obvious that I found in sound a most effective qualification of the visual world. A street became *informed* for me by the sounds of a barrel-organ. Everything had a new angle of light upon it, a new arrangement with a centre pulsating like a heart. Thus the street was not only organized; it became an organism, it came alive. The images of dismemberment and anxious aridity that haunted me were not in this way dissipated: but an element of drama, even of "healthy" catastrophe, was a relief. Aided by the pictures on my father's cigar boxes and on the barrel-organ and by visits to the pantomime, that distant, anglicized cousin of the *Commedia dell'Arte* theatre, the music in the street could provide me with a variety of scenes, populated, Baroque, catastrophic.

It is now a Neapolitan tune the Italian grinds; which says: the tall casa has painted shutters and each window a painted rococo entablature, brown upon the pink stucco of the wall. Families cluster at the rickety balconies. A man beats a carpet; the flotsam floats and swims in the sunlight towards the gay washing hanging below. Under the roof there is a broad band of fresco. (Gigantic mermaids wreck the fisher boats and tritons blow blue horns.) In a window a birdcage dangles. At first I think there is but one bird, but the hops are now frequent and I see the cage is over-populated. The tiny movements are so vivid that the great damp sheets which hang from the side of the balcony appear grey, and the bundle between the iron bars, not a little girl. You were young then too, and over the clambering terraces of houses, each with a flat square roof, you had arranged a cord that joined you to my house, a little higher up on the other side of the valley. By jerking this cord we could exchange exciting messages, words which the roar of the mills on the brook between could not silence. Inside the room is bric-a-brac, particularly ornamental feathers dusty with canary seed. The breeze softly lifts the light wooden frame of a mirror on the wall. As you jerk the cord, sirens are screaming in the harbour, tugs scurry and hoot, white figures below labour with sacks of flour while, above, smoke rises straight and blue from the black volcano.

The tune changes . . . Sometime the old men sat upon the mountain, each upon a stone seat. Their heads touched the blue sky. Night clattered on in valleys below and over night's invisible back a portent leaped. Another darkness, a cloud of ashes, over-whelms the feeble day. Some jump from terrace to terrace; from vineyard and from vineyard, mothers round up their children, moving like Hecubas; while below upon the lowest road the fire of the dying sun draws scarlet bands about the feet of fugitives, is now extinguished by dust, now clutches at a cart upon whose frame winnowing petals open . . . a cart among the rain of ashes and overtaken women bundled into fantastic attitudes: a cart, on and on, carts piled with toppling bric-a-brac crowned by sobbing children, by basket and spring that last saw the full light of day strong in the early market: on and on to the sea that rises from the bosom of a gully ahead like a gown that opens its velvet grasp and leaves the shoulders bare. Cruel, even sea, you throw no rescue ropes. Uprooted olive trees festoon the road as it rocks.

Light of this last day is butchered by lava and steam: yet, every now and then, a bloody ray of seared sun-fire shoots among the fugitives.

We survivors, as we approach the gully, look back and there, sure enough, above the black of the earthquake and of the vapour, above the well-established night that glows red with illicit warmth, the old men sit agleam against a blue sky. In this cursed double night they still possess the day. Surely we wake to their tomorrow when at dawn, stiff after dead sleep upon the deck of the rescue ship, we pluck the morning air and search with sudden glance the shimmer of the cold and velvet deep . . .

It is noticeable that not only were these fantasies provoked by sound but contain in them the projection of a great deal of noise. Even the scenes of my early childhood sustained their life through movement, the circulation of traffic. Where there is movement there is noise, and from the noise we fashion images of movement.

In our urban life, sound qualifies visually scenes which otherwise are confusing and meaningless to the eye. What the eye alone might perceive is inhuman to a degree. The arts today concerned with interrelationship of sound and movement, particularly ballet, are able to draw upon a wealth of life-giving fantasy which in one form or another is common to millions.

Thus, the barrel-organ did not restore in the fullest sense the visual world for me. Such was my anxiety and consequent ambition that it could be satisfied with nothing less than an instantaneous, silent manifestation, independent of sound and of a dramatization of the passage of time: a happy co-existence, then, of things in space after the manner of mensa the table. It is possible, following an older habit, that the intrusion of sound will still provide a *point d'appui*, but it will nevertheless be serving an entirely different effect.

As the train came out of the Mont Cenis tunnel, the sun shone, the sky was a deep, deep, bold blue. I had half-forgotten about my table for more than ten years. At once I saw it everywhere, on either side of the train, purple earth, terraces of vine and olive, bright rectangular houses free of atmosphere, of the passage of time, of impediment, of all the qualities which steep and massive roofs connote in the north. The hills belonged to man in this his moment. The two thousand years of Virgilian past that carved and habituated the hillsides did not oppress; they were gathered in the present aspect. At the stations before Turin, the pure note of the guard's horn but sustained and reinforced the process by which time was here laid out as ever-present space.

We arrived at Turin in the late afternoon. There was a change-with a wait of half an hour. On a low platform in the clean electric space – shadowless, it would seem – I stood enraptured. I watched the sky between the trains and the edge of the huge gradual curve of the station roof. The sky was now a paler blue but was still close, like the near sound of trumpets.

Day gave way to night without misgiving. Soon, in the new train, it was entirely dark. Although for the last hours of the year, the air was soft, tender, a darkness as of a perfect-fitting lid. After dinner in the restaurant car, most of the passengers had left, the tablecloths were removed. On the other side of the gangway, one table ahead, I again saw the mensa table. Not the plain deal table, it is true. But two Italians sat there with instant faces. Between them in a fiasco was the wine, and to my ears they talked like Romans. Their warm precipitation of life sustained, as it seemed to me, by the glowing reflected light of thousands of sunlit years, banished memories of Hyde Park. Instead of the Serpentine, I saw the Mediterranean, the end of my journey. In their eyes I read the pleasure of housetops and of different levels.

We were in an electric train. While we stopped at Genoa, I could imagine a giant taut city above the Mediterranean. A young man with a red scarf escorts his sweetheart to the train. He is ugly, but he, too, holds in his eyes the pleasure of the housetops and the different levels: of alleys between towering painted walls that float in the shade like goldfish in the sunlight.

The train began to move through Genoa. I could see through the many lighted windows of clear-shaped tenements. In every apartment, I felt, there is this happy evening return, a state of the night which is sheer acquisition; in which, like the men in the train, the inhabitants take up the night by expending the strength of a Latin day. Their talk is now the balustrades, the terraces, the balconies spread out upon the harbour, the radiant open places of the town. The ebb and flow of conversation, still more, of gesture, reconstruct the thoroughfares. As the train glided on, more and more peep-shows appeared at every angle to the line. The inhabitants had no need for blinds; since no dominant misery and no surfeit of unexpressed emotion lurked inside them, there was nothing beyond the houses to be shut out.

Meanwhile in a straight passage the train was passing houses on every level to the line, now above them, now on a level with the second storey, now at the foot, now crossing a great viaduct. I had the sensation of passing through the inside as well as along the outside of the houses; never before had I been so much at home. There was every kind of light, perhaps a darkness except from the windows, perhaps a lit campo with ever-bustling happy trees tenacious of root, silent and soft, or a terraced garden with an easy iron gate and steps upon the prospect. There was a conspiracy abroad of universal triumph informing even the roads, the pavements and the harshest stucco. And when we stopped at stations beyond Genoa, at Nervi for example, and finally at Rapallo, the air held scents of flowering trees and of eucalyptus enclosing and disclosing the villas mounting on their gardens. I drove in a carriage through the town to the pension. Echoes of the horses' hooves upon the cobbles brought with them from the walls a sensation of their diurnal brightness. At the end of the ride, the horse was walking up a steep incline through the garden to the pension, a large Riviera villa set behind a balustrade. The scents intensified; there was the sound of waters falling to the sea. Church bells began, and then rang out from every side, from overhanging levels as well as from distances; swift, hammering, light bells. It was midnight, the new year.

On waking in the morning I saw through the open French windows, over the top of a russet-red villa with green shutters, the Mediterranean, the place-name of our civilization. There was a revealing of things in the Mediterranean sunlight, beyond any previous experience; I had the new sensation that the air was touching things; that the space between things touched them, belonged in common; that space itself was utterly revealed. There was a neatness in the light. Nothing hid or was hidden. Soon, an electric train passed, gliding with ease on the hard way just below, entered a tunnel. Unlike the electric trains on London's metropolitan railway which had always been a disturbance, this train and the tunnel did not prolong themselves inside me. It seemed that for the first time things were happening entirely outside me. Existence was enlarged by the miracle of the neat defining light. Here was an open and naked world. I could not then fear for the hidden, for what might be hidden inside me and those I loved. I had, in fact, incorporated this objective-seeming world and proved myself constructed by the general refulgence. Nothing, for the time, lurked, nothing bit, nothing lurched.

As I think now of that valley at Rapallo that goes up to Mont Allegro, as I think of the afternoon winter sunlight, I have the sensation of a sound which contains every note, prolonged, entirely sustained, as good beneath as above, a sound that provides every aural want; at the same time it is itself the epitome of complete realization. Nature spreads and mounts before me, fixed and growing, changeless in the clearness of its cycle. I have here the means of action, a demonstration, not of the purpose of life but of the power of life to be manifest; not of one thing but of the calm relationship of many things, concrete things, each bound to each by an outwardness that allows no afterthought to the spectator: an outward showing goes within him. An answering life wells to the surface, and he feels – hence the great beauty of Mediterranean landscape – that the process of a man's existence is outward, giving shape, precise contour to the few things that lie deepest; whatever the distortion they mutually endow, making the expenditure in terms of a surface we call expression, be it in action, art or thought.

The outside world, our own bodies, other people and material things point the goal of outwardness. The Mediterranean scene invokes the universal aim. In adult life, my models have been things rather than persons.

But whatever the degree, whatever the distortion, all men impute themselves to their surroundings. The broad distorted aspect of the innermost informs every particle of the huge outlying space.

Even a sense of duration or succession discovers itself occasionally as a simultaneity, as forms arranged in space. I do not think that a more direct account of my relations with people would reveal as much as this sparse account of a contemplative relation with the external world. Doubtless it is a proof of neurosis. It determines, however, without prejudice, the aesthetic aim to cause surroundings to describe matters less immediate, perhaps, but often more profound than are revealed by reminiscences; further, to illustrate (given the biological essence) that the human process is aesthetic in so far as it is outlined against the beckoning outwardness of the external world.

Of course it is basic human relationships, above all, that my two landscapes describe. Hyde Park is especially a destroyed and contaminated mother, Italy the rapid attempt to restore. In their terms, and it would seem to me in their terms alone, could I re-create succinctly the division, the incorporation of opposites.

Envoi [ii]

Again we must reach a new communion between the inner and the external worlds. This time it is a godless outside world. We are would-be gods in a godless world.

Give all over to science. It is the way of truth, the only way to peace of mind. And science will grow to proportions even more monstrous, monstrous that is, were they to be seen by the eyes of our generation uneasy and miserable in a half-way house amid a

---

ii   From "Envoi" to *Venice: An Aspect of Art*, 1945; *Critical Writings* II, 134-138.

world afflicted. Give over everything to science without a qualm. For a new glory illumines the imaginative life, a purer imaginative life whence it is conceived and called so after the victories of science. Yet it will be this imaginative life, aesthetic "truth", fantasy, which will define by contrast the truth of science. Let us not be frightened to apply that word "fantasy" to what we value most. Fantasy cannot be undermined if utter devotion is also paid to truth. The most profound object of contemplation is the relationship of fantasy with reality, between the partial and the impartial. To make the distinction absolute, to value both of its terms, will be the highest achievement of man.

The longer flights of fantasy, of course, attain aesthetic "truth". Science and art, that is all, prose and poetry: and what a relief it is, the release from mumbo jumbo of every kind, from the prose-poetry of the ages which wears miserably thin, weft and warp tearing each other.

It will be asked: what of religion?

The belief in durable good is essential to well-being. Bereft of it altogether we die. The original essence is a belief in the efficacy of love. We need a sense of optimism almost at the centre of our beings if we are to sleep well. It is far more important to us than truth. How much truth can be borne? We know, all of us, or are capable of knowing apart form the compulsion of neurosis, that religion is simply not true. But can we do without it, and if so, how? For assuredly in everyday life and in certain situations in particular, the feeling of ultimate solicitude is indispensable, even if the strength that ensues is not much drawn upon. It is at worst a shield from exposure to Nature in the raw.

The only way to do without religion or without any substitute rationalization is to welcome and foster the original sense of interior goodness both as a fantasy and as a fantasy that corresponds with the very working of life: for there is only love and death, and it behoves living creatures for their welfare to carry deep inside them the love of love. It is possible and desirable, then, to subsist on something nearer the original impulse rather than on its more extensive rationalization which so often challenges truth and so often is paralysed by truth. Any dogma makes impossible demands upon the intellect. The private myth, known to the owner as a myth, can possess something of the beauty of organized religion, although for the most part it is voiceless and incommunicable. In future ages it will be seen that the ordinary man's conceptions of his mother, in her good and bad aspects, are, where formulated, more profound, more touching, more poetic than all the systems and dialectics of Good and Evil. It may be found that the belief or trust in the good object inside, as one might call it, entails some degree of aversion from reality. Some degree of dissociation in personal matters would seem inevitable.

Now, I would not claim that such belief in the good inner object can equal the pervasiveness of living religion which possesses a god or gods who walk the earth, where the outside world is dizzy with an actual presence and with the miracle involved. Such exteriorization carries the familiar process in a most dramatic form. Still, much meaning is destroyed; much prosaic meaning is lost in the zest for an all-consuming poetry. And this same poetry soon settles down into a dull and distorting and enslaving prose-poetry, the greatest of all shackles on human progress. We too must exteriorize the internal object. We must follow the process of life knowingly, and the more willingly; above all, the more consistently. Because of its falsehood, too much evil is done in the name of religion. But for us, the death instincts will play a smaller part in our exteriorization of love except admittedly as servant. Where they equal or are stronger than the love instincts, there could not be any further pretence of a belief in a good object, since the belief is directly inspired by the feeling of a good object that varies in strength and must, therefore, perennially be renewed at the fount: unlike religious belief which, for the most part, is divorced from religious experience. And even religious experience is often dominated by fear and sense of guilt rather than love. The good object, too, no doubt, is largely built upon a foundation of guilt feeling. It is there to fill the frequent void. Without it we should be at the mercy of our aggression. Nevertheless it is a good object, it is a repository of love and generosity, not the propounder of guilt feeling as are so many religious doctrines. For religion, not seeing the compulsion to possess a good object to counter hate – a compulsion, shared by every human being, from which all religions grow – always overstates the case and is therefore confronted by what Christianity calls "the problem of evil". To meet this problem, and also because an amount of arrogance and sadism finds expression in dogma, the stress is shifted to guilt.

We are today in a position to reverse the ontological argument for the existence of God, one of the oldest and most potent of all the Christian arguments. The ontological argument says that since man finds within him the idea of God, therefore God must exist: there can be no other explanation for man's conceiving of divinity. But we are in a position to say that since we harbour the idea of a good object (i.e. God), and since without it we should very soon die, it is a contradiction to conceive this power to be also outside us. Indeed, the essence of the fantasy is that the good object lives at the root of our imagination rather than in Nature, the universe, the outside world known to science that opposes itself to fantasy, and by which it is contrasted and defined. It is we who are the gods in a godless world. And as it is with God, so it is with the Devil.

The world revealed by science cannot satisfy emotion. At great cost man has learned to defer his pleasure at the behest of the reality principle. Let the principle have full stature: the deeper satisfactions are then beyond its reach. Such true knowledge would only strengthen aesthetic fantasy so that they make each other poignant. Moreover, so huge is our partiality that all impartial thought is noble and sublime as well as useful. And the will to perpetuate, the compulsion to project in fantasy an ideal settlement of things, have their content and their beauty in the realization of an indifferent universe. So vast our partiality, it makes with the pressure of the indifferent universe, an aesthetic balance, provides all meaning with an aesthetic tang. Since it is his mode to suppress, to sublimate, to discover reality and then to project, only in the setting of natural law a to which all phenomena, including himself, are subject, may man measure and contemplate in completeness man's desire. I should say, the rest of man's desire, since some part of feeling finds expression in impartial thought.

There is, then, again today a pungent dualism, as in the days of Giorgione, a more vivid current, as it were, passing between the poles of subject and object. Fantasy requires fact and vice versa. The uneasy masquerade of a frenzied fact is played out. We will seek truth and "aesthetic truth"; we will increase the importance of art.

For we come to realize that artistic creation – and this point has been stressed over and over again – is the epitome of all living processes. Stimuli conjoin as a pattern; action no less than utterance obtains its definite form from the mental flow. Within the terms of a particular stimulus the whole of man's experience is expressed anew each moment of consciousness, just as in art the patterns of the mental life are made known through the data of the senses. Like a work of art, consciousness is a kind of concentrating reflector of the manifold spirit. By means of the perspective of a particular stimulus, every aspect has a place, however minute. There proceed ceaselessly correlation, rationalization, distortion. Always, something is expressed in terms of other things. Substitution is the constant factor of mental activity. To create is to substitute. Consciousness is made up of reality sensations and of substitutions, of reality and its image. Man is alive twice over: he has the power both to live and to enlarge upon living. He is alive in reality and in image.

With the aid of reason, man constructs images from the ceaseless material of a few primary emotions. Each fresh composition uses anew the material of all previous structures. To me it is strange that no mystique has attached itself to this process.

Every philosophy is based upon an opposition of terms. Its aim is either to describe their interaction and find the absolute in the interaction or combination itself, or else to reduce the one to terms of the other and thereby create an absolute. It is worthwhile to contemplate in a way that philosophers have not done before philosophizing, the generic pair of opposites in which our lives are cast. The newborn baby soon becomes aware that neither his mother nor the surrounding world is an extension of himself. Henceforth, to his dying day, there remains the huge division between himself and objects, people or things. Throughout life we seek to rival the externality of things. The world as we perceive it, our animal habitat, is the language of every passing mood or contemplative state. Indeed, without this canvas, as it were, on which to apply ourselves, by which we project and transmute as well as satisfy more direct biological needs, we cannot conceive the flow of the mind any more than the activity of the body. The body is obviously meaningless without a further external world; but so too is the mind. Mental as well as physical life is a laying out of strength within, in rivalry, as it were, with the laid-out instantaneous world of space. To project is to distort. From moment to moment we can look upon the truth within only in terms of an outside ramification, taking for our arrangement the exquisite arrangement of space.

We carry with us all the time the certainty of life and of death, a relationship parallel to the interdependence of subject and object. We strive to manifest our living (subject) in rivalry with the laid-out dispositions of the outside world. In the end, we do indeed in death (object) become solely a part of the inert outside world. As well as defining each other, our conceptions of life and death supplement each other. It is not surprising to find that the activities of intellect are supplementary, in the pursuit of fact for the purposes of practical life and of science, and in the construction of fantasy: "objective" and "subjective" respectively in character. The fearless allocation, and thereby the further satisfying of these two activities, is the proper study of mankind.

I repeat: it is obvious that fantasy should not have part in science. Yet it has done in all thought anterior to science, has blocked the emergence of science for thousands of years. All emotional expression is rationalized: that is the very breath of our life. But if we use the word truth where there is partiality, it must be in the sense of "aesthetic truth". Our images are compounded of fact and of reason, vast rationalized structures that hold in duress the fluid emotions. Images encase thought and are articulated by thought, but they are not primarily the products of thinking. Consciousness is no more of the mind than the surface is of the sea. And just as the surface of the sea lies opposite to the sky and, indeed, is thus defined, so does consciousness lie opposite to the external world. Mental processes, unknown in themselves, obtain entry to consciousness through speech. Symbolic substitution, even before speech, is natural to the infant. The basis of speech is substitution, the basiz of all projection. To create is to substitute.

The external world is the sounding-board of the emotions. That is self-evident: nevertheless, in contemplating the eternal poetry of Giorgione's *Tempesta*, it has seemed a discovery.

Donald Meltzer[i]

On 15 December 1972, in a lovely terraced Georgian house in Church Row, the most beautiful street in Hampstead, the country playground of eighteenth-century London, Adrian Stokes (1902–1972) died quietly and with great dignity, painting to the very last despite the impairment from brain metastases of a rectal carcinoma. His life was both a private and a public one of unflagging devotion to art and to psychoanalysis – and to building a bridge between the two that will stand for generations.

He was born in London and educated at Rugby and Magdalen College, Oxford. Handsome and sociable, a superb tennis player and gifted speaker, his life was equally divided between the scholarship of art history, painting, and participation in the worlds of art and psychoanalysis. He numbered many of the most distinguished figures of both worlds among his personal friends: Ezra Pound, Naum Gabo, D. H. Lawrence, Roger Money-Kyrle, Ben Nicholson, Barbara Hepworth, and many, many others. He served the Tate Gallery

---

i "A biographical note on Adrian Stokes", *Contemporary Psychoanalysiz* (1974), 10: 342-345.

for several years and saved the work of the Cornish primitive, Alfred Wallis, from destruction at the time of the artist's death in poverty and obscurity. He was among the first patients of Melanie Klein when she came to England, and this experience coloured his life and activities thereafter. In 1950, with the musician Robert Still, he founded the Imago Society of London.

However, painting and writing about art were his two main professional activities. He published twenty books and many papers in journals of art history and psychoanalysis. His paintings, mainly landscape early on, still life of bottles later, and nudes finally, are widely appreciated and hung in many collections. So much then for his status. To define his stature is less simple, for his thought was deep, his aesthetic intuition sure, and his mode of expression poetic, but not easy. His chief areas of study were the Russian ballet, art and architecture of the Italian Trecento and Quattrocento, painting of the impressionists, and culture of the Greeks. From this mélange, with the aid of psychoanalytic theories, chiefly those of Melanie Klein regarding the child's preoccupation with the inside and outside of the mother's body, he fashioned an aesthetic theory. Although its evolution was slow and its eventual structure never expounded, it has been pulled together in Professor Richard Wollheim's edition of a collection or rather selection of the works of Mr Stokes, *The Image in Form* (1972).

In might be interesting to chronicle my personal experience from private conversations, dinner parties, visits to galleries with him, and the period during which he helped me to write the section that I contributed to *Painting and the Inner World* (1963). To Adrian Stokes emotion was the central phenomenon of mind, and art the central record of emotion in civilization. When he embraced psychoanalysis, and the developments of Melanie Klein's thinking, in particular, he did so because the theories seemed to him to throw an unparalleled light on the phenomenology of art as what Wittgenstein has called "a form of life". While he decried the psychoanalytical tradition initiated by Freud in papers such as *Leonardo, Gradiva,* and *Dostoyevsky,* in which the personal aspect of the content of the work was placed above its formal structure in importance, he felt that the understanding of unconscious mental processes *in general* gave a new and richer meaning to the formal aspects of the creative effort. He thus was inclined to seek for the mysterious powers of art in its basic references to bodily experience and object relations, to visual configurations (*Colour and Form*), tactile sensations (*Smooth and Rough*), to the geography of life space (*Inside Out*), and to the haunting quality of repetition of patterns, the "incantatory" element, as he called it.

Adrian Stokes' approach to understanding this medley of configurated phenomena held as its basic reference the body of the child and his unquenchable thirst for knowledge about his body, and that of the mother, who was both his "world" at the outset, and his template for the larger world later on. Like Melanie Klein's early emphasis on the role of the "epistemophilic instinct" in the development of the child's mind, Stokes always laid stress on the exploratory aspect of looking and listening, the way in which the eyes and ears have fingers to touch, a nose to smell, a tongue to taste the aspects of the world they encounter. Thus for him a painting was first of all a surface which the artist variously attacked and caressed, and which the viewer fairly crept about on with his eyes. He held that this exploration followed two great modes of operation, that of breaking into (carving) and that of restoring (modelling), corresponding to the activities of the child in its relations to the mother, first aggressively entering her under the sway of its impulses in disregard of her welfare (paranoid–schizoid position) followed by attempts to repair the damage its unbridled needs had produced (depressive position). The constant operation and oscillation of these two processes was as necessary for the development of a work of art as it was for the evolution of mental structure in the child.

In consequence of this emphasis on the thirst for knowledge, art and science were absolutely fused in Adrian Stokes' view, and must be fused if creative work was to supplant mere skill. It seemed to him absolutely natural that Piero della Francesca should have been interested in mathematics, for

Newton to be a theologian, and for Wittgenstein to be a musician. Nor did he ever doubt that in the most skilled hands, a cultured mind could make both a science and an art form of psychoanalysis. Had other interests not called him so urgently and other talents not so early found their means of expression, he would have made a splendid psychoanalyst. He was a splendid man.

Eric Rhode[i]

F ar from being Olympian, Adrian Stokes was among the
most hospitable of men: alert to distress in others and
willing, at considerable cost to himself, to be of help;
both receptive to ideas and able to enjoy the pleasures of small
talk. But even on a first meeting with him it became clear
that the essential Stokes was a very private person. He was
involved in some communion with himself that could not
be intruded into; at the same time, and in no manner, could
this communion be ignored. It shone forth in his aspect: in
crowded rooms his look of vulnerable nobility set him apart.
And its richness spilled out in conversation, as in his sometimes obscure stating of a viewpoint that fascinated by the
breadth of its connections, or in the lucid, casual remark that
could cut to the quick of an argument. He had nothing to do
with what he describes in one of these papers as the "unceasing expostulation" of polite society.

It would be natural, yet too limited, to see the content of his
thought in terms of his life-long allegiance to the arts or, more

---

i "Introduction" to *A Game That Must Be Lost* (Stokes, 1973), pp. 1-5.

accurately, to the idea of art itself. Two memories throw light, perhaps, on the varied intensities of this allegiance. On the opening morning of the great Matisse retrospective, held at the Hayward Gallery in 1968, he seemed overwrought, even wild – like some young man about to take out his beloved for the first time. However, on a later visit to the National Gallery he gave every sign of being at home. We wandered among the Venetians. Whenever he made an observation on the paintings, as when he referred to Titian's deftness in suggesting the contours of an old man's shoulder, he did so sparely. His pleasure was intimate. Although he sometimes wrote about art as a kind of theology, he declined to see the process of making or appreciating it as hierophantic. They were both embedded in practicality, as robust as agriculture and not entirely dissimilar. In much the same way as he distrusted the motives of artists who work everything up into a frenzy, he sensed the envy underlying the post-Romantic idealization of the artist that attends so much modern publicity.

But his communion extended beyond art, or even the most sensitive forms of aesthetic response, to the widest concern with wholeness and the ways in which intelligence can bring together sensation and thought. Indeed, the theme that threads together these papers, so that each reinforces the other, gently delineates the intricacy of this communion, consisting as it does of a contemplation on the nature of contemplation.

In "Primary process, thinking and art",[ii] where he explores this theme most explicitly, he argues that to dissociate the kind of thinking that goes on in the making and appreciation of art from reasoning can diminish the miraculous complexity of both activities. To view art, on the one hand, as a playground where regressive states of mind can be exercised and reasoning, on the other, as a "completely logical or realistic attachment to reality" (and in this context, he asks, what do we mean by reality?) either denies the corporeity and omnipresence of unconscious phantasy or denies the existence of an inner life altogether, as in those

---

ii See extract above, Chapter 1.

rigid and overcontrolled types of thinking that sometimes (and misleadingly) go by the name of reasoning.

"The question is whether reasoning itself, as a process, is shorn away from the rest of the mind." Stokes not only acknowledges, in a quotation from one of R. E. Money-Kyrle's essays, that the power to differentiate, so crucial to reasoning, comes into play at the same time, if not before, the capacity for displacement and condensation (two of the mechanisms ascribed to the primary process: the logic of whose operations, it has been thought, is primitive in the sense that it evades the exigencies of the human predicament), but he also demonstrates that art as a cultural institution is, like culture itself, "witness to an unceasing concern, whatever the reasonableness of which we are capable, with inner life", that "visual perception, in particular, involves a sorting out, a grasping, of relevant differentiation" as subtle and yet as forceful as the most impressive kinds of reasoning. Art, he writes, "revivifies, enlarges upon, the link between all mental and active apprehensions of outside things together with their introjections."

In later years, and with characteristic generosity, he did entertain the possibility that some of his ideas might have been transposed into a more accessible style. In all fairness to him, though, it should be added that his wish to apply psychoanalytic concepts to art was in keeping with the wide-ranging idea of intelligence that he had acquired from the psychoanalyst Melanie Klein, which he both celebrates in these papers and develops by the emphasiz he places on the paramount importance of contemplation. No aspect of experience need be excluded by contemplation, he surmised; and no one was less touched than he by the Shavian notion of intelligence as a walking head. As a young man he had been an athlete, and he was always aware that to separate the integration of the athlete or ballet dancer from any definition of intelligence could only weaken that definition. While working for long periods at his paintings, he found it helpful to take time off to watch sports programmes on television: the grace of the footballer or tennis-player, he used to say, strengthened his capacities for co-ordination. And he liked to tell of how Ben

Nicholson and he used to be stimulated, when playing billiards, by the changing patterns of the balls on the green baize.

In the opening section of this book he covers three subjects that, at first sight, seem disconnected: the unconscious physicality and shapeliness inherent in the least sensitive use of language; some of the reasons why social conventions are so restricted; and the significance of certain ball games. Yet in each case he shows how aesthetic contemplation – which for him was the most unforced way of experiencing the blossoming of thought, perception and feeling – could discover a common source in these different themes. He enacts what he means by contemplation in "Form in art", a paper first drafted in 1931 and revised many times. While evoking the Rembrandt portraits in the National Gallery, he lays stress on the muscular response that comes about with the correlating of vision and sees this movement towards integration as mobilizing and bringing together some of the least accessible aspects of the mind. But he defines the quality of this integration most succinctly in "Primary process, thinking and art" when he describes how a scientist, that popular representative of reasoning at its most abstract, considers a landscape:

> His thoughts before the landscape are by no means circumscribed with considerations of strata or density of population. The shapes at which he looks, whatever the object of his immediate attention, are bound to encounter the inner landscape. I have not in mind here the perception of a phallic symbol, say, in a tree, but the impingement of the total configuration as a symbol, an aspect of symbolization *vis-à-vis* the outside world at large, to which psychoanalysts are not inclined to pay prolonged attention.

His Tavistock Press series of books has investigated some of the ways by which art distils this process. He thought that the contemplation of art encourages the spectator to recognize the "total configuration as a symbol" through the structure of what he called "the image in form". And he believed that the contemplation of art, even more than the contemplation of landscape, could bring the spectator to an intuitive understanding of how the often inchoate self might identify with those internal figures that psychoanalysts call "good objects". Works of art, he maintained, derive many of their attributes from the ability of both artist and spectator to commune with such objects. Neither work of art nor good object coerce; they invite. They envelop us while at the same time remaining other. Ugliness, on the contrary, is strident. One of the reasons why "bad smells" offend polite society, he argues, is that they overpower, stifle, do not allow us the possibility to discriminate.

By seeing how the act of disinterested contemplation reinforces our identification with all that we find inspiring and good he was able, through an understanding of the wide meaning of this identification, to bring a range of unexpected allusion into his thought. Many readers coming to his writing for the first time are most impressed by the wit of these allusions without quite recognizing how securely they depend on argument. Yet he was being more than fanciful, or even perceptive, when he recalled that "the smell of Madeira cake can be identical with the smell of cold roast chicken" or that "it is to drink in with conflict a sunny day that a crowd arrives at Lords: for cricket seems to make the day even sunnier, and similarly the width of sky, the size of green." The act of contemplation, he proposes, always carries with it the poignancy of renunciation as well as an undertow of conflict. It is far from the "good form" of polite society where "average conventional behaviour keeps before us a dulled image of the good and bad, the one muddied by the other. If the bad can be held in strict restraint, so can the good." It is far from the "good form" of the sportsman: too often the "good loser" in sport screens "the danger of absolute loss with the easy acceptance of conditional loss." An important concern in the three essays on the death instinct, that make up the second part of this collection of papers, is indeed to show how the act of contemplation is related to the capacity for bearing "the danger of absolute loss". The death instinct, he surmises, is more than an aggregate of the destructive impulses in the self; it has its own life-giving component. He sets great store on the possibility that

> ... in all life-giving and life-preserving responses there is mingled an impulse, however faint, of refusal, in virtue of which no creature needs to be taught about death ... I think that from the

very beginning the impulse of refusal is felt within other instinctual responses and tends to increase them, as might a slowly departing train the response of a man who would catch it.

Against calculation, feelings of triumph or indifference and other denials of loss, he places the experience of resignation, the sense of reconciliation with one's lot, most vivid when we contemplate:

> We shall have found that a beloved place never looked so beautiful as at the moment when we had to leave it, probably for ever . . . To gaze at the garden is no longer to include in the impression our concern: the moment has come when the struggling flower or weed demonstrates fully a singular peace. All perfection is close to death . . .

To wish to die at a moment of fulfilment contains the thought, perhaps, that in so dying it is we who depart and leave the scene undisturbed.

Readers of the Tavistock Press books will have realized that in the last years of his life Stokes' views on the future of art, technology and the community were bleak. He thought there was little hope. At the same time he acknowledged that the impending threat of his own annihilation distorted perception and he treasured the little hope he could perceive. His last sustained piece of writing "The future and art", first addressed as a lecture to young audiences in Camberwell and Chelsea, discloses how in spite of all conflict he was able to hold onto a steadiness that neither counselled despair nor (and it can be equally cruel as advice) manic utopianism. "Maybe even the journeys to the moon will prove to have fixed our feet the more firmly on this various planet." As the final days of his life ebbed away, he told many of his friends of his newly found peace of mind: he had rediscovered, with an added conviction, that this beloved place never looks so beautiful as at the moment when we have to leave it.

Bann, S. (2007). (Ed.). *The Coral Mind: Adrian Stokes's Engagement with Architecture, Art History, Criticism, and Psychoanalysis.* University Park: Penn State Universisty Press.

Bion. W. R. (1967). *Second Thoughts: Selected Papers on Psychoanalysis.* London: Heinemann.

Carrier, D. (1997). Ed. and introduction. *England and Its Aesthetes: Biography and Taste: Essays by John Ruskin, Walter Pater, Adrian Stokes.* Amsterdam: Overseas Publishers Association.

Carrier, D. & Kite, S. (2002). Eds. and introduction. A. Stokes, *The Quattro Cento and Stones of Rimini.* Farnham: Ashgate.

Clark, K. (1949). *Landscape into Art.* London: John Murray.

Freud, S. (1900). *The Interpretation of Dreams. S. E.,* 4–5.

Freud, S. (1915). *The Unconscious. S. E.,* 14: 166-204.

Freud, S. (1925). Negation. *S. E.,* 19: 235-239.

Freud, S. (1941 [1938]). Findings, ideas, problems [marginal notes]. *S. E.,* 23: 300.

Glover, N. (2009). *Psychoanalytic Aesthetics: An Introduction to the British School.* London: Harris Meltzer Trust.

Gowing, L. (1978). (Ed.). *Critical Writings of Adrian Stokes.* 3 vols. London: Thames & Hudson.

Graziani, R. Adrian Stokes and the psychoanalytic. *Adrian Stokes.* http://www.pstokes.demon.co.uk.

Hulks, D. (2001). Painting, atom bombs and nudes: symbolism in the later psychoanalytic writings of Adrian Stokes. Journal of Psychoanalytic Studies, 3 (1): 95-109.

Langer, S. (1942). *Philosophy in a New Key: A Study in the Symbolism of Reason, Rite, and Art.* Cambridge: Harvard University Press.

Lewin, B. D. (1948). Inferences from the dream screen. *International Journal of Psychoanalysis,* 29: 234-241.

Kite, S. (2008). *Adrian Stokes: An Architectonic Eye.* Leeds: Legenda.

Kite, S. (n. d.). The affirmation of the eye. *Adrian Stokes.* http://www.pstokes.demon.co.uk.

Klein, M. (1957). *Envy and Gratitude: A Study of Unconscious Forces.* London: Hogarth Press.

Klein, M., & Rivière, J. (1937). *Love, Hate and Reparation.* London: Hogarth Press.

Meltzer, D. (1973). *Sexual States of Mind.* Perthshire: Clunie Press. Reprinted Harris Meltzer Trust, 2008.

Meltzer, D. (1974). A biographical note on Adrian Stokes. *Contemporary Psychoanalysis,* 10: 342-345. Reprinted in this volume, Appendix 1.

Meltzer, D. (1983). *Dream Life.* Perthshire: Clunie Press. Reprinted Harris Meltzer Trust, 2008.

Meltzer, D., & Stokes, A. (1963). Concerning the social basis of art. In: A. Stokes, *Painting and the Inner World,* pp. 19-46. Reprinted in D. Meltzer & M. H. Williams, *The Apprehension of Beauty.* Perthshire: Clunie Press, 1988.

Milner, M. (1950). (1950). *On Not Being Able to Paint.* London: Heinemann.

Milner, M. (1955 [1952]). The role of illusion in symbol formation. In: P. Heimann, M. Klein & R. E. Money-Kyrle (Eds.), *New Directions in Psychoanalysis.* London: Tavistock; reprinted in M. Milner, *The Suppressed Madness of Sane Men* (1960), pp. 234-240.

Money-Kyrle, R. E. (1968). Cognitive Development. *International Journal of Psychoanalysis,* 49: 691-698. Reprinted (with postscript) in D. Meltzer (Ed.), *The Collected Papers of Roger Money-Kyrle.* Perthshire: Clunie Press, 1978.

Read, R. E. (1988). "Art today": Stokes, Pound, Freud and the word-image opposition. *Word and Image,* 14 (3), 227-252.

Read, R. E. (2002). *Art and its Discontents: The Early Life of Adrian Stokes.* University Park: Penn State University Press.

Read, R. E. (2012). Vico, Virginia Woolf and Adrian Stokes's autobiographies: fantasy, providence and isolation in post-war British aesthetics. *Art History,* 35 (4): 778-795.

Rhode, E. (1973). Ed. and introduction. *A Game That Must Be Lost: Collected Papers of Adrian Stokes,* pp. 1-5. Cheshire: Carcanet Press. Reprinted in this volume, Appendix 2.

Sayers, J. (2000). *Kleinians: Psychoanalysis Inside Out.* Oxford: Polity Press.

Smith, P. (2002). Wittgenstein, description, and Adrian Stokes (on Cézanne). In: P. Smith & C. Wilde (Eds.), *A Companion to Art Theory*, pp. 196-214. Oxford: Blackwell.

Stokes, A. (1925). *The Thread of Ariadne.* London: Kegan Paul

Stokes, A. (1926). *Sunrise in the West: A Modern Interpretation of Past and Present.* London: Kegan Paul.

Stokes, A. (1932). *The Quattro Cento: A Different Conception of the Italian Renaissance.* London: Faber & Faber. New edition: D. Carrier & S. Kite (Eds.), *The Quattro Cento and Stones of Rimini.* Farnham: Ashgate, 2002.

Stokes, A. (1934). *Stones of Rimini.* London: Faber & Faber. New edition: D. Carrier & S. Kite (Eds.), *The Quattro Cento and Stones of Rimini.* Farnham: Ashgate, 2002.

Stokes, A. (1934). *Tonight the Ballet.* London: Faber & Faber.

Stokes, A. (1935). *Russian Ballets.* London: Faber & Faber.

Stokes, A. (1937). *Colour and Form.* Revised edition, 1950. London: Faber & Faber.

Stokes, A. (1945). *Venice: An Aspect of Art.* London: Faber & Faber.

Stokes, A. (1947). *Cézanne.* London: Faber & Faber.

Stokes, A. (1947). *Inside Out: An Essay in the Psychology and Aesthetic Appeal of Space.* London: Faber. Reprinted in D. Carrier (Ed.), *England and Its Aesthetes: Biography and Taste: Essays by John Ruskin, Walter Pater, Adrian Stokes.* Amsterdam: Overseas Publishers Association, 1997.

Stokes, A. (1949). *Art and Science: A Study of Alberti, Piero della Francesca and Giorgione.* London: Faber & Faber.

Stokes, A. (1951). *Smooth and Rough.* London: Faber & Faber.

Stokes, A. (1955). *Michelangelo: A Study in the Nature of Art.* London: Tavistock.

Stokes, A. (1956). *Raphael: 1483-1520*. London: Faber & Faber..

Stokes, A. (1958). *Greek Culture and the Ego: A Psychoanalytic Survey of Greek Civilization and of Art*. London: Tavistock.

Stokes, A. (1958). *Monet: 1840-1926*. London: Tavistock.

Stokes, A. (1961). *Three Essays on the Painting of Our Time*. London: Tavistock.

Stokes, A. (1963). *Painting and the Inner World (including a dialogue with Donald Meltzer)*. London: Tavistock.

Stokes, A. (1964). Living in Ticino. *Art and Literature*, 1: 232-238.

Stokes, A. (1965). *The Invitation in Art*. London: Tavistock.

Stokes, A. (1967). *Reflections on the Nude*. London: Tavistock.

Stokes, A. (1972). *The Image in Form: Selected Writings*, ed. R. Wollheim. Harmondsworth: Penguin.

Stokes, A. (1973). *A Game That Must Be Lost: Collected Papers*, ed. E. Rhode. Cheshire: Carcanet Press.

Stokes, A. (1978). *Critical Writings*, ed. L. Gowing. 3 vols. London: Thames & Hudson.

Stokes, A. (1981). *With All the Views: Collected Poems*, ed. P. Robinson. Worthing: Littlehampton Book Services.

Williams, M. H. (1988). Holding the dream: the nature of aesthetic appreciation. In: D. Meltzer, D., & M. H. Williams, *The Apprehension of Beauty*, pp. 178-199. Perthshire: Clunie Press. Reprinted Harris Meltzer Trust, 2008.

Williams, M. H. (2008). A post-Kleinian model for aesthetic criticism. *PsyArt Journal*. http://www.psyartjournal.com/article/show/harris_williams-a_post_kleinian_model_for_aesthetic_crit.

Wollheim, R. (1965). Preface. A. Stokes, *The Invitation in Art*. London: Tavistock.

Wollheim, R. (1969). The mind and the mind's image of itself. *International Journal of Psychoanalysis* 50: 209-220.

Wollheim, R. (1972). Ed. and introduction. *The Image in Form: Selected Writings of Adrian Stokes*, pp. 9-31. Harmondsworth: Penguin.

Wollheim, R. (n. d.). Introduction: *Adrian Stokes*. http://www.pstokes.demon.co.uk.

Mozart, W. A. 42
musical qualities/sound 13, 63,
    69, 76, 91, 128, 142
  in poetry 108
  and speech 3, 21–22
naturalistic art 10, 30, 42, 67, 71,
    73, 84, 109
nature xvi, 8, 17, 48, 62, 67, 95,
    98, 108, 111
  as mirror of man 112
  see also inner and outer
    worlds
nude, as art form 35, 37–38, 57,
    64, 113, 156
Nicholson, B. 75, 155
object, aesthetic/psychoanalytic
    passim, xvi, xvii, 22, 27, 76,
    124
  bad/destroyed 45, 64, 66
  and capacity for love 4, 6
  corporeal nature of 30
  first (breast) 114
  fragmentation/splitting 5, 19,
    27, 38, 68, 114
  good/restored xvi, 41, 45, 47,
    48, 71, 150–151, 162
  image of 10, 26, 79
  independence/otherness of
    xiii, xviii, 14, 18, 32, 34,
    40, 46, 63, 75
  intact/whole 44, 56, 73, 84,
    114, 119
  internal qualities xiv
  minimum 5, 7
  relating to xxii, 4, 36, 38, 39,
    41, 64, 72–75, 101, 104,
    109, 157
  see also imago; mother;
    part-object
oceanic feeling 14, 43
  see also merging with the
    object

otherness/outwardness xiii, xix,
    14, 32, 34, 47, 61, 63, 68,
    71, 79, 81, 92, 101, 133
  aspiration toward 104, 112,
    147, 148
  and compulsion 12
  and contemplation xxii
  and fusion xvii
    see also object, independ-
      ence of
part-object relations xiv, xvii, xviii,
    5, 17, 30, 33, 44, 46, 69
  see also object
persecutory anxiety 4, 5, 7, 20,
    34, 47, 81
  excessive 18
perspective 58, 75, 99ff, 123, 141
Picasso, P. 40, 43, 59
Piero della Francesca xxiv, 53,
    99ff, 111, 157
  and "family of things" 104
  geometry in 103
Platonism xxiii, 64
poetry 14, 73
  and aesthetic truth 149
  diction of xxiv, 22, 25, 69
  incantation of 63
  of myth 88
  and the reader 72
  synthesis 107–108
positions (Kleinian) see depressive
    position
post-Kleinian theory xiv, xix
preconception, innate xxiii, 19
primary process xvii, 16, 19, 21,
    26, 161
projective identification see intro-
    jective and projective identi-
    fication
psychoanalysis passim
  and aesthetic experience xiii,
    27, 39